Contents

When you've completed each project, give yourself a star!

I like this page best.

GAMES

Coding with Scratch Made Easy

Learn the Basics, Games, and Projects

Written by

Jon Woodcock & Steve Setford

DK

Written by
Steve Setford & Jon Woodcock
Editors Radhika Haswani, Steve Setford
Canadian Editor Barbara Campbell
Designer Peter Radcliffe
Art Editor Kanika Kalra
Jacket Designer Dheeraj Arora
Managing Editor Soma B. Chowdhury
Art Director Martin Wilson
DTP Designer Dheeraj Singh
Producer, Pre-Production Dragana Puvacic
Producer Priscilla Reby
Publisher Sarah Larter
Publishing Director Sophie Mitchell

First Canadian Edition, 2016
DK Canada
320 Front Street West, Suite 1400
Toronto, Ontario M5V 3B6
First published in Great Britain by
Dorling Kindersley Limited.

ISBN 978-1-55363-274-0

DK books are available at special discounts when purchased in
bulk for corporate sales, sales promotions, premiums, fund-
raising, or educational use. For details, please contact
specialmarkets@dk.com

Printed and bound in China

Scratch is developed by the Lifelong Kindergarten group at
MIT Media Lab. See http://scratch.mit.edu

A WORLD OF IDEAS:
SEE ALL THERE IS TO KNOW

www.dk.com

What is Scratch?

A computer doesn't have a smart brain like you, so everything you want it to do must be broken down into lists of simple instructions called programs. Giving instructions to the computer is known as programming, or coding.

What you'll learn:
• To do tasks, computers need simple instructions called programs
• Scratch is a great place to start programming
• What the ingredients of a Scratch project are

What does a computer understand?

Instructions for computers have to be written following special rules and using only words the computer understands. These words and rules make up a "programming language." There are lots of different programming languages. Many have funny names, such as JavaScript, C++, and Python.

A program is a list of instructions for the computer

What is Scratch?

Scratch is a computer programming language that's easy for beginners to use. In Scratch, programs are made by joining together coloured blocks using the mouse. These groups of blocks (called scripts) tell characters on the screen (called sprites) what to do. Scratch is free, safe, and fun to experiment with.

The blocks fit together like jigsaw pieces

Scratch projects

With Scratch, you can make your own interactive stories, animations, games, music, and art. Scratch has large collections (or "libraries") of graphics and sounds, as well as sprites and backdrops that you can play around with. Let your imagination run wild—you'll soon pick up the coding skills you need!

We can make lots of sounds!

What makes up a Scratch project?

Here's a Scratch project. Think of it like a play. The action takes place in an area called the stage. The "actors" (the sprites) are controlled by lists of instructions (the scripts). Behind is the backdrop —the "scenery," which can be changed.

Click the green flag to run (start) a program

Click the red button to stop a program

Backdrop (background picture)

Add a script to make the shark sprite move

Sprites are used for all the objects we want to move or control

This is the stage

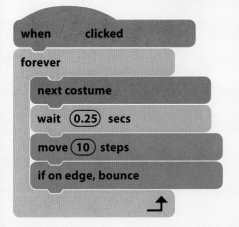

Scripts for sprites

This is an example of a script. It makes the shark sprite bounce around the stage, opening and closing its mouth. Each block gives an instruction to the sprite. A block might tell a sprite to move, change how it looks, talk in speech bubbles, react to other sprites, or make a sound.

Show what you know
Fill in the spaces to practise the key language of Scratch.

1. A .... is a set of instructions (program) in Scratch.

2. Objects that perform actions in a project are called ....

3. In a Scratch program, the action takes place on the ....

4. Starting a program is called .... it.

5. A collection of sounds or graphics is called a ....

Getting Scratch

You can code online at the Scratch website, but if you aren't always connected to the Internet, you can install it on your computer. Ask a grown-up to help you. **You will need the newer Scratch 2.0 for this book, not the old Scratch 1.4.**

What you'll learn:
• You need Scratch 2.0
• How to use Scratch on a computer
• How to join the Scratch website
• How to save your projects

Using Scratch online

If you register for a Scratch account, you will be able to save your projects online and share them with friends.

1 **Sign up for Scratch**
Go to **scratch.mit.edu** and select **Join Scratch** for instructions on how to register. You will need to get permission from an adult with an e-mail address.

2 **Create in Scratch**
When you want to use Scratch, go to the Scratch website and click on **Create**. This will open the Scratch editor window.

Click on this file to see your saved projects

3 **Save in Scratch**
Projects save automatically if you're logged in to your Scratch account. You can see your saved projects by clicking on the file with an **"S"** at the top right of the screen.

S

Top tip from Scratch Cat

Need to "right click" but only have one button on your mouse? Usually you can hold down the control (**CTRL/ctrl**) key or shift key on the keyboard as you click. Not working? Then ask the owner of the computer.

Installing Scratch on a computer

If you don't have access to the Internet or you want to work offline, you'll need the Scratch installer. Go to **scratch.mit.edu/scratch2download** and just follow the installation instructions.

To start Scratch, just double-click the **Scratch 2.0** icon on your desktop.

Double-click the **Scratch 2.0** icon to start

Operating systems

Check that your computer's operating system is able to run Scratch.

● The online version of Scratch 2.0 will run on Windows (PC), OS X (Macs), and some Linux computers.

● The offline version might not work with some Linux computers.

● The Raspberry Pi can't run Scratch 2.0 at the moment.

You're not in this book.

Scratch online community

On the Scratch website you can share your projects and try out other coders' Scratch creations. Even better, you can explore how every project works and even change ("remix") them. Look out for the buttons shown below.

Let's explore Scratch!

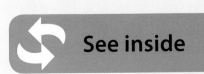
See inside

Remix

Exploring Scratch

Open Scratch on your computer and this is what you'll see. All you need to create and run your Scratch projects is on this screen. Take a look around.

Experiment!
• Click the buttons and tabs to experiment with Scratch. Don't worry, you won't break the computer!

Change language

Save projects here

Delete sprite or script

Help tool

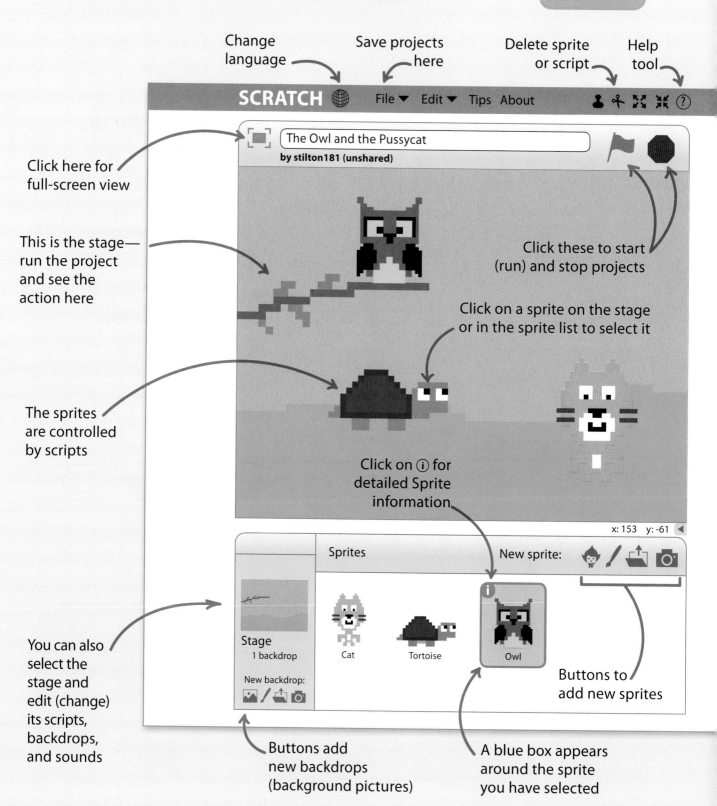

Click here for full-screen view

This is the stage— run the project and see the action here

The sprites are controlled by scripts

You can also select the stage and edit (change) its scripts, backdrops, and sounds

Click these to start (run) and stop projects

Click on a sprite on the stage or in the sprite list to select it

Click on ⓘ for detailed Sprite information

SCRATCH   File ▼   Edit ▼   Tips   About

The Owl and the Pussycat
by stilton181 (unshared)

x: 153   y: -61

Sprites   New sprite:

Stage
1 backdrop

New backdrop:

Cat   Tortoise   Owl

Buttons add new backdrops (background pictures)

A blue box appears around the sprite you have selected

Buttons to add new sprites

▶ Scratch map

The stage is where projects are run. The sprite list shows all the project's sprites. Script blocks can be found in the blocks palette. Build scripts in the scripts area.

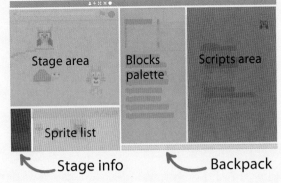

Stage area | Blocks palette | Scripts area

Sprite list

Stage info

Backpack

Costumes tab—use this to change a sprite's appearance

Sounds tab—use this to change the sounds a sprite makes

Click here for step-by-step guides and tips

Scripts tab

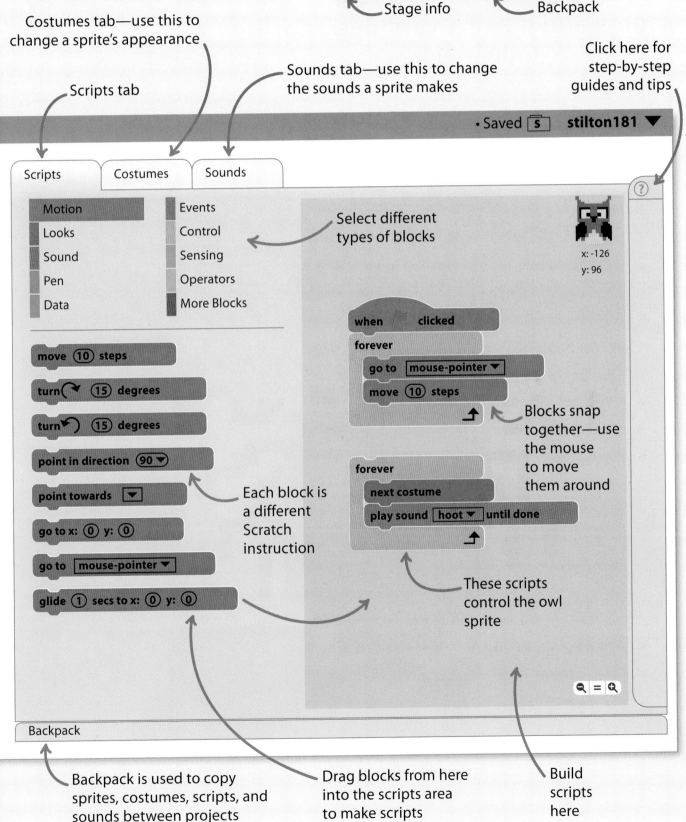

• Saved ⟦S⟧ **stilton181** ▼

Scripts | Costumes | Sounds

Motion
Looks
Sound
Pen
Data

Events
Control
Sensing
Operators
More Blocks

Select different types of blocks

x: -126
y: 96

move (10) steps

turn ↻ (15) degrees

turn ↺ (15) degrees

point in direction (90 ▼)

point towards (▼)

go to x: (0) y: (0)

go to mouse-pointer ▼

glide (1) secs to x: (0) y: (0)

when ◼ clicked
forever
　go to mouse-pointer ▼
　move (10) steps

forever
　next costume
　play sound hoot ▼ until done

Blocks snap together—use the mouse to move them around

Each block is a different Scratch instruction

These scripts control the owl sprite

Backpack

Backpack is used to copy sprites, costumes, scripts, and sounds between projects

Drag blocks from here into the scripts area to make scripts

Build scripts here

Learn the Basics

Do you know how to build a script, create a loop, and make an animation? Don't worry, in this section you'll learn all this and more. Let's get programming!

Let's explore Scratch!

Your first project

Time for our first Scratch project. We're going to create some simple instructions to make the cat talk. By moving the coloured blocks around with the mouse, we can build a simple computer program called a script.

What you'll learn:
- Sprites are controlled by scripts
- How to build a script from Scratch blocks
- Things in scripts happen one block at a time from the top
- You can read Scratch to find out what it does

▶ Scratch—the friendly cat

First, open the Scratch editor: either choose **Create** on the Scratch website, or click the Scratch icon on your computer. You'll see the cat sprite standing on the stage. Let's make a script to tell the cat what to do.

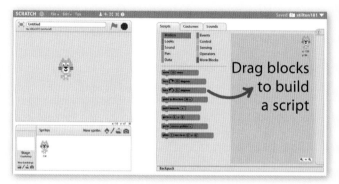

Drag blocks to build a script

Click on the **Looks** label

1 Start a new script
We'll begin by getting the cat to say a friendly "Hello!" Click on the purple **Looks** label under the **Scripts** tab in the centre of the editor.

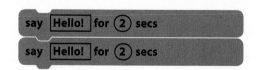

2 Select a say block
The list of blocks in the middle of the editor will change. Click with the mouse on the top **say Hello!** block and drag it to the right, into the scripts area.

say Hello! for ② secs

3 Do it again!
Drag a second **say Hello!** block into the scripts area. Release the mouse button when the blocks overlap, so that they lock together like jigsaw pieces.

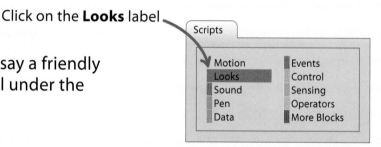

say Hello! for ② secs
say Hello! for ② secs

4 Change what the cat says
We can tell the cat to say something different. Click on the lower **say Hello!** box in the stack. Type in a new message, such as "Nice day!"

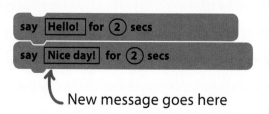

say Hello! for ② secs
say Nice day! for ② secs

New message goes here

Brown event block clips on top of speech blocks

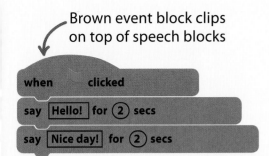

5 Completing your script
Click on the brown **Events** tab. Drag the top brown block in the list to the right, into the scripts area. Hover it over the top **say** block, then let go of the mouse button. The brown block will clip on to the two purple **say** blocks.

Clicking the flag runs the script

6 Read the whole script
The script tells us that to start things off we need to click on the green flag in the top right corner of the stage. This is called "running" the script.

Hello!

2 seconds

Nice day!

2 seconds

7 Watch the action
When you click on the flag, Scratch Cat will say "Hello!" for two seconds. Then it will say "Nice day!" for two seconds.

See how the blocks work in order—the cat does each action in turn.

8 Save it!
Good job! You've built your first Scratch project! Save it by clicking on the **File** menu and choose **Save** or **Save All**.

Scratch puzzle
We've picked some blocks for our cat to try out. Draw a line from each block to the correct picture of what the cat will do.

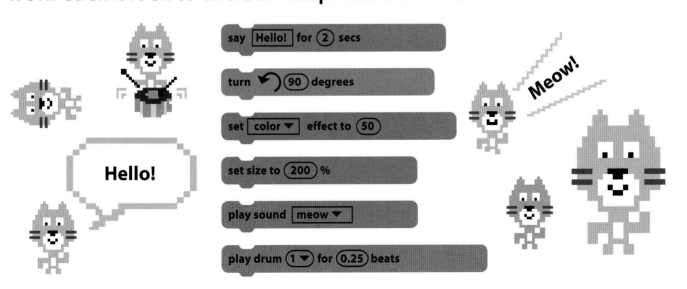

Move it!

Now for some action. Let's get our cat moving using the dark blue **Motion** blocks. Scratch measures distances in "steps." The stage is 480 steps wide and 360 steps tall. There is a block to stop sprites from getting stuck to the walls. They just bounce off them!

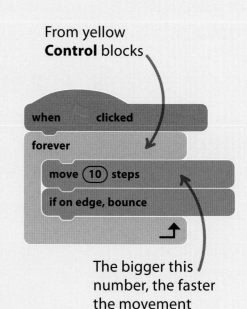

What you'll learn:
• How to make a sprite move
• That Scratch measures distance in steps
• How to keep sprites the right way up

▶ Let's move the cat

Start a new project. Click on **File** above the stage and select **New**. Add this script and think about what the blocks do.

Click the green flag to run the script. The cat will move a short way to the right. Try it a few times.

Click on the **10** in the **move** block and type **100**. The cat now moves much further each time. Experiment by trying different numbers of steps.

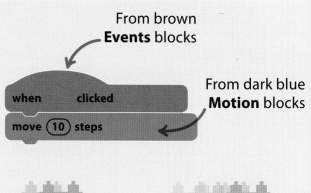

From brown **Events** blocks

From dark blue **Motion** blocks

when clicked

move 10 steps

10 steps

100 steps

▶ Bouncing off the walls

Now change your script to this. Read the script. What do you think it does? The **forever** block repeats the blocks inside—forever! The **if on edge, bounce** block turns the cat around at the edge of the stage.

Run the new script. The cat will now run right, then left, across the stage. Experiment —the more steps there are in each move, the faster the cat goes.

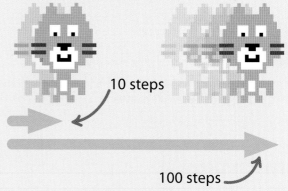

From yellow **Control** blocks

when clicked

forever

move 10 steps

if on edge, bounce

The bigger this number, the faster the movement

▶ Stop standing on your head, cat!

The poor cat spends half its time upside down—how awful! To stop this, click on the blue ⓘ in the corner of the cat in the sprite list. Extra information about the sprite appears. Change **rotation style** to <->. Try the other rotation styles to see what the cat does.

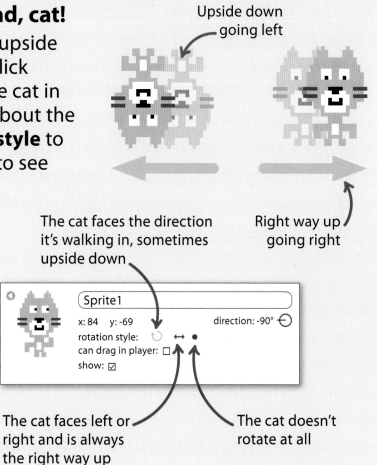

Upside down going left

Right way up going right

The cat faces the direction it's walking in, sometimes upside down

Click here to get information about the sprite

The cat faces left or right and is always the right way up

The cat doesn't rotate at all

Show what you know
How far can you go with this quiz? All the way to the end?

1. What colour are the **Motion** blocks? ....

2. Scratch measures distances in units called ....

2a. How many of these units wide is the stage? ....

2b. How many of these units tall is the stage? ....

3. A mistake in a program is known as a "bug."
This script should make the cat move across the stage slowly, but when I click the green flag to run it, nothing happens! What's wrong?

....
....
....
....

```
forever
  move (2) steps
  if on edge, bounce
```

We love bugs!

Which way?

When you want to move a sprite, you need to know two things: how far and which way. Every sprite has a built-in direction arrow. When a script gets to a dark blue **move** block, that's the direction in which the sprite will go.

▶ Cat follows mouse!

Let's spin our cat around in every possible direction. Open a new project in the Scratch editor. Build this script for the cat sprite. Read the script. What do you think it does? Click the green flag to see if you guessed correctly.

Move the mouse-pointer around the stage and watch the cat turn around so it always looks toward the pointer. The **forever** block runs the **point towards mouse-pointer** block over and over.

From brown **Events** blocks — From yellow **Control** blocks — From dark blue **Motion** blocks

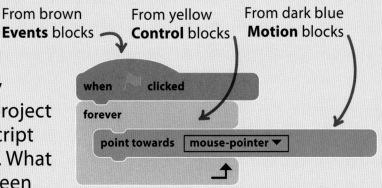

when [ ] clicked

forever

point towards [mouse-pointer ▼]

The cat will follow the mouse-pointer

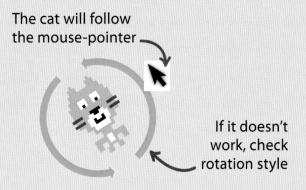

If it doesn't work, check rotation style

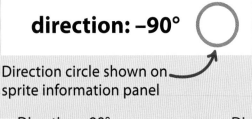

direction: −90°

Direction circle shown on sprite information panel

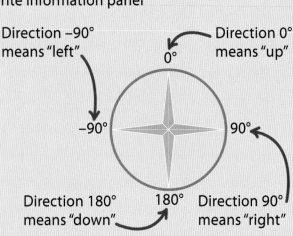

Direction −90° means "left"

Direction 0° means "up"

0°

−90°

90°

Direction 180° means "down"

180°

Direction 90° means "right"

◀ Sprites know where to go!

Every sprite knows what direction it's pointing. A sprite's direction is shown in the sprite information panel when you click the blue ⓘ.

As the cat spins around, you'll see its direction value change and the blue line pointer move around the direction circle.

Use the "compass" shown here to decode the direction number.

▶ Choosing a sprite's direction

We can also set a sprite's direction using the window on the **point in direction** block. You can click on the little triangle beside the number for useful directions, or just click on the window and type in a number.

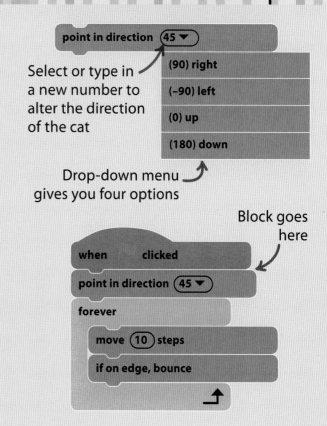

Select or type in a new number to alter the direction of the cat

(90) right
(–90) left
(0) up
(180) down

Drop-down menu gives you four options

▶ Bouncing off the walls again

Add the **point in direction 45** block to the "bouncing off the walls" script from page 16. Put it after the **when green flag clicked** block but before the **forever** block. Run the script. The cat will set off diagonally. Try using different directions and rotation styles.

Block goes here

when clicked
point in direction (45 ▼)
forever
    move (10) steps
    if on edge, bounce

Show what you know
Know your way around Scratch? Then try these brain teasers!

1. What number should replace the **?** in this block to set the sprite's direction to:

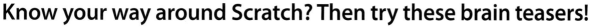
point in direction (? ▼)

Up = ...

Left = ...

Down = ...

Right = ...

2. Test your Scratch script reading powers! What does this script do? Read it carefully and try to act out each block in your mind.

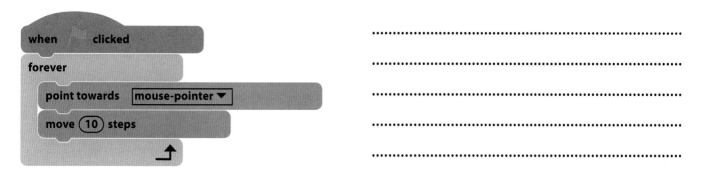

when clicked
forever
    point towards mouse-pointer ▼
    move (10) steps

....

....

....

....

....

Loops

In computer programs, we often want to carry out the same instructions more than once. To avoid having to put down the same blocks many times, we can wrap them in a loop instruction that repeats the blocks. Meet **forever** and **repeat** loops!

▶ Running down the blocks

Start a new project and make this script. Read, understand, and run it. It runs very quickly and doesn't do much.

When we run the script, each block is run in turn from top to bottom. First the cat turns a little, then the cat's colour changes to green.

▶ Forever loops

A loop instruction runs a script in the normal order from top to bottom, but then loops back to the top. The loop runs the blocks inside over and over again. Try wrapping a **forever** loop around the blocks from the last script.

Now the cat turns more and changes colour each time the blocks in the **forever** loop are repeated.

Press the red button to stop the loop.

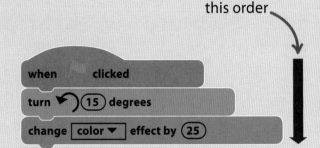

Blocks run in this order

I feel a little sick!

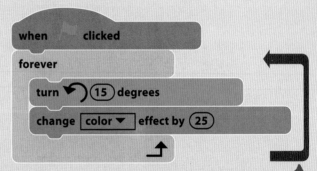

When the actions finish, the program always goes back to the start of the loop

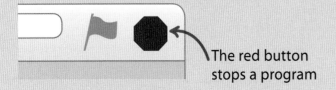

The red button stops a program

Help! I'm in a spin!

▶ Repeat loops

If we want to repeat a group of blocks only a few times and then move on to the rest of the script, we can use the **repeat** loop block.

Try this script for a siren that annoys the cat. The **repeat** loop runs the two **play note** blocks 10 times and only then runs the **think** block. Try changing the number of repeats.

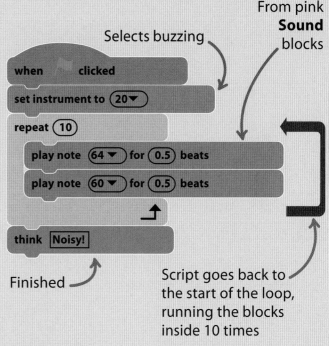

Selects buzzing

From pink **Sound** blocks

Finished

Script goes back to the start of the loop, running the blocks inside 10 times

That really is noisy!

You're not kidding!

Show what you know
What do you know about loops? Test yourself with this quiz.

1. Loops are used to .... groups of blocks.

2. Two types of scratch loops are .... and ....

3. You can stop a **forever** loop by clicking the ....

4. In which section do you find the pink blocks? ....

5. Which block section has the loops in it? ....

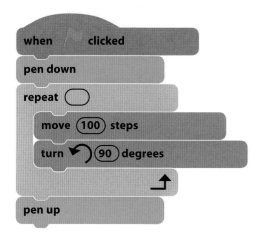

6. Bug hunt! This script should draw the four sides of a square, but nothing happens when it's run. Can you spot and suggest a fix for the bug? Programmers call this "debugging."

....

....

....

Animation

The characters in cartoons seem to move, but really you are just watching lots of slightly different pictures that fool your brain into seeing movement. This is called animation. Sprites can be animated in the same way.

What you'll learn:
• How to animate sprites
• Sprites can change how they look
• How to use costumes
• How to load new sprites from the Scratch library

Costumes tab

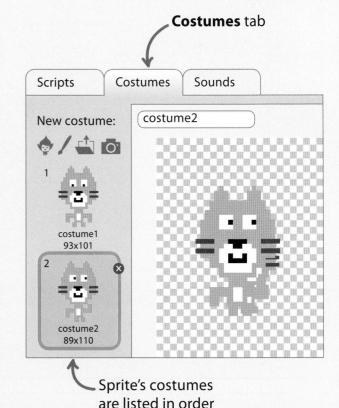

Sprite's costumes are listed in order

▶ Changing costumes

Our cat sprite has two different pictures, or "costumes," it can show. Start a new scratch project and click on the **Costumes** tab just above the block list. You will then see the two costumes the cat sprite can "wear."

▼ Walking the cat

To animate the cat, build and run this script. The **forever** loop repeats the **next costume** block. The picture of the sprite changes every half second, and this makes the cat look like it's walking. Try adding a **move** block in the loop to improve the animation.

This picks the next costume

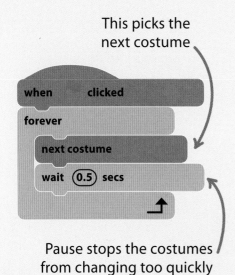

Pause stops the costumes from changing too quickly

Quickly swapping costumes makes it look as if the cat is walking

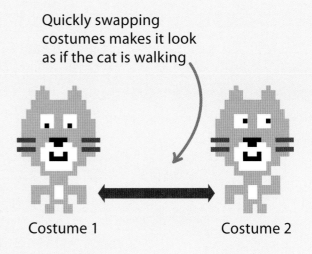

Costume 1   Costume 2

▶ Dancing ballerina

You can use this same script to get other sprites dancing! Let's add the ballerina sprite to the project. Click on **Choose sprite from library** at the top of the sprite list. Then select the ballerina and click **OK**.

New sprite:

Choose sprite from library

Click on the first icon to see all the sprites

Add the costume-changing script to the ballerina's scripts area. She has four costumes. Click on the **Costumes** tab to see them. When you run the script, she uses them all as she dances on the stage.

Look! I'm dancing!

Let's have a party!

◀ Sprite party!

Try adding lots of dancing sprites to your project. Choose sprites with two or more costumes. Try Dinosaur1 or some of the dancing kids.

Show what you know

You can make sprites dance. Can you solve these problems too?

☆

1. A different picture a sprite can show on the stage is a ....

2. .... is showing pictures with slight differences in order to make a sprite appear to move.

3. Can you rearrange the sprites below to animate a jumping pony?

Write the numbers 1 to 5 in the boxes to show the correct order.

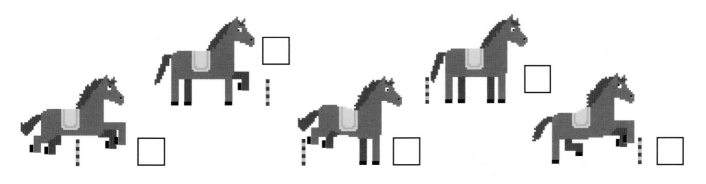

Party time!

We've learned a lot about making sprites do things, but a project isn't complete if it happens on a silent, white stage! Let's see how to give a project some scenery and music from the Scratch libraries to liven things up.

What you'll learn:
• How to change the background picture
• How to add effects to the backdrop
• How to add music to your project

"party" stage

▶ Adding scenery—backdrops

Just as a sprite can have many costumes, the stage too can have more than one background picture, or backdrop. Click on the **Add new backdrop from library** button at the bottom left of the stage info area.

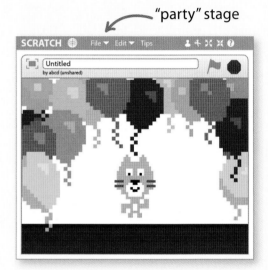

It's Scratch Cat's birthday, so choose the "party" stage. You'll see the cat on the stage! You can load more than one backdrop. Try loading "underwater2."

You can switch the backdrop in any script using the **switch backdrop** or **next backdrop** blocks from the **Looks** section.

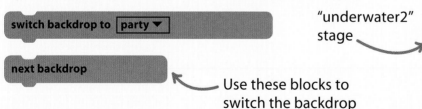

switch backdrop to party ▼

next backdrop

"underwater2" stage

Use these blocks to switch the backdrop

▶ Light show!

We can add scripts to the stage: click on the small picture of the stage area at the top of the stage info area. Then try running this script with your party backdrop to bring it to life.

Continually changes the colour of the stage

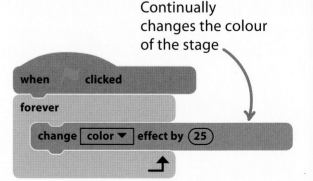

when   clicked
forever
   change color ▼ effect by 25

▶ Music

A party isn't a party without music! Sounds can be loaded into a sprite or the stage. But you must make scripts to play them in the scripts area.

Clicking on the speaker under the **Sounds** tab will take you to the **Sound Library**

1 **Load some music**
Click on the stage again. Then click on the **Sounds** tab above the blocks and select **Choose sound from library** (the speaker symbol).

2 **Select a tune**
Choose one of the music loops, such as "dance funky," and click **OK** in the bottom right corner to load. The sound will appear on the list of sounds.

Choose your groove!

Plays the whole sound before going to the next block

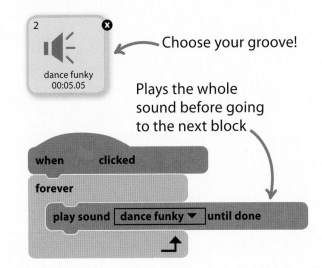

3 **Make, read, and run a script**
Click on the **Scripts** tab and make this script. Read the script and run it. You should have never-ending music!

Show what you know
The cat's in the mood for a party. Are you in the mood for a quiz?

1. A background picture on the stage is called a ....

2. Circle the block that plays a whole sound before continuing:

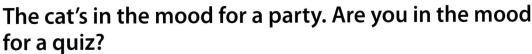

3. True or False?

a. A project can have only one backdrop loaded. ....

b. Only the sprite that loaded a sound can play it. ....

c. The stage can have sounds and scripts. ....

d. Once you've chosen a backdrop for a script, you can't change it. ....

e. A sprite can use a script to change the stage's backdrop. ....

if-then

If it's raining, then we decide to wear a raincoat. We can make this kind of decision in Scratch using the **if-then** blocks from the yellow **Control** section. Like loops, they wrap around other blocks and control when they are run.

Spin control

Let's use **if-then** blocks to decide when our cat spins. We'll use some light blue **Sensing** blocks, which ask a "true or false?" question. Find them under the **Scripts** tab.

Sensing block goes into window at top of **if-then** block

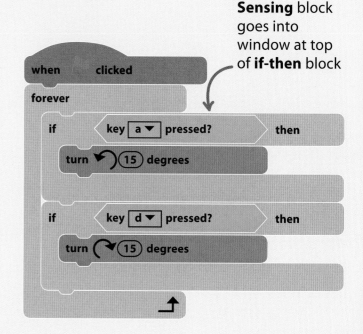

1 Start a new project
Add this script. What do you think it does? The block inside each **if-then** block is only run if the answer to the question at the top of the block is "true."

Cat turns 15 degrees to the left

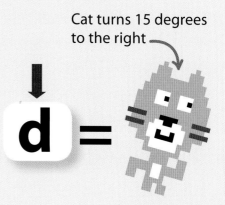

2 Run the script
What happens? Nothing! Press the **"a"** key and the cat turns backward. Let the key go and it stops. The **turn** block inside the first **if-then** block is only run when the answer to the question **key a pressed?** is "true."

Cat turns 15 degrees to the right

3 Now press the "d" key
The cat turns the other way. The **turn** block inside the second **if-then** block is only run when the answer to the question **key d pressed?** is "true." If neither key is pressed, then both **turn** blocks are skipped.

A closer look at the if-then block

Look at this **if-then** block taken from a script. Read it carefully and think about what it does.

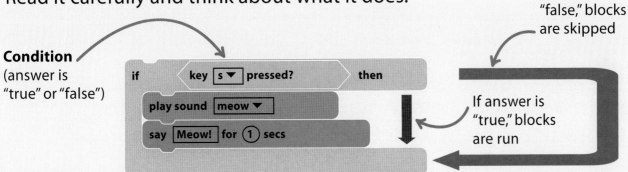

If answer is "false," blocks are skipped

Condition
(answer is "true" or "false")

if ⟨ key [s ▼] pressed? ⟩ then
   play sound [meow ▼]
   say [Meow!] for ① secs

If answer is "true," blocks are run

- The **if-then** block is a yellow **Control** block, because it controls when blocks inside it are run.

- An **if-then** block has a question known as a **condition**. The question must have a true/false answer.

- The blocks inside the **if-then** block are only run when the answer to the question is "true."

- If the answer to the question is "false," then the blocks inside the **if-then** block are ignored.

- Add this **if-then** to your script so the cat meows when you press the **"s"** key. Put the **if-then** block inside the loop but outside the other **if-then** blocks.

Press that key down!

S

Meow!

Show what you know

If you're a Scratch expert, then you'll find this bug hunt easy!

This script should make the sprite change colour when you press the space key, but the sprite changes colour all the time. Can you spot the "bug"? ....
....
....

when ⚑ clicked
forever
   if ⟨ key [space ▼] pressed? ⟩ then

   change [color ▼] effect by ㉕

Variables

Computers are excellent at storing information, or "data." This data could be someone's name or the weight of a cake in a competition. A variable is like a labelled box in which you can store data until your program needs it.

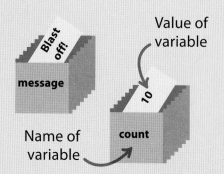

Value of variable

message

Name of variable

count

A box with a label

A variable can store a number or some words (programmers call words a "string"). The thing stored in a variable is called its value. You can change the value of a variable. Give variables helpful names to make the code easy to read.

Follow these instructions to create your first variable in Scratch.

1 Start with data
Select **Data** under the **Scripts** tab. Then click on the **Make a Variable** button. The **New Variable** window will pop up.

Select **Data**   Click on the **Make a Variable** button

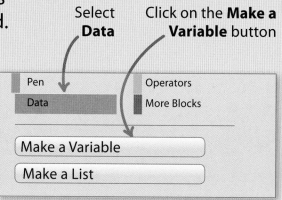

Pen   Operators

Data   More Blocks

Make a Variable

Make a List

2 Name it, check it, click it!
First, give your variable a useful name. Check **For all sprites**, and click **OK**. (You can ignore the **For this sprite only** box.)

New Variable

Variable name: count

● For all sprites   ○ For this sprite only

OK   Cancel

3 Get to know your blocks!
Blocks for this variable will then appear in the blocks area. Make sure you know what each of the blocks does.

Check to show the variable on the stage

The variable block can be used inside other blocks

This block gives the variable a value

Increase the variable's value using this block (a negative number decreases the value)

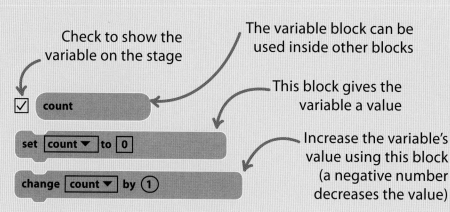

☑ count

set count ▼ to 0

change count ▼ by ①

▶ Countdown cat

Time to see some variables in action. Start a new project.

In the orange **Data** section, create two variables called **count** and **message**. Always give your variables names that explain what's stored in them.

Add this script. Make sure you drag the little orange blocks with **count** and **message** on them into the windows of the **say** blocks. Don't type the words into the **say** block windows. If you do, the cat will say the variable's name rather than what's stored in the variable.

Read the script. Can you work out what's going to happen? Now run the script.

Experiment with the numbers and text in the script. Can you make the cat count up instead of down?

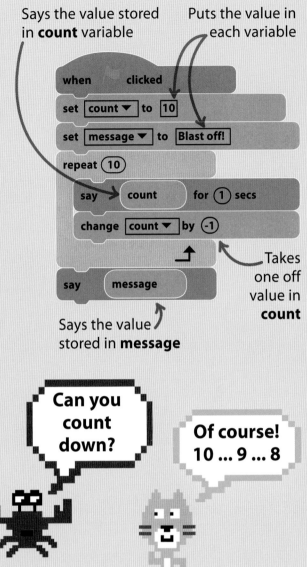

Says the value stored in **count** variable

Puts the value in each variable

Takes one off value in **count**

Says the value stored in **message**

Can you count down?

Of course! 10 ... 9 ... 8

Show what you know
Test how much Scratch data you've stored in your brain-box.

☆

1. A variable has a name and a ....

2. Make a Variable button is found in the orange .... blocks section.

3. Fill in the speech bubbles for these sets of blocks:

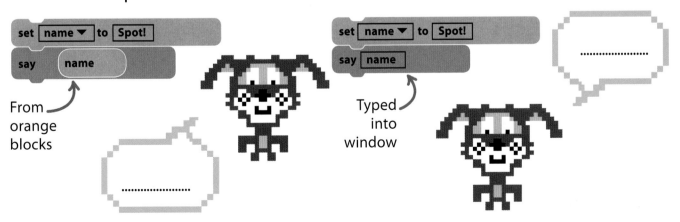

From orange blocks

Typed into window

Math

Scratch can do all the math you know about. But some of the symbols it uses are different, to fit with what's on your computer's keyboard. We can do equations in Scratch and use variables in them. Scratch can even roll dice for us.

> **What you'll learn:**
> • How to do math in Scratch
> • What math symbols computers use
> • How to do equations with variables
> • How to "roll dice" using the computer

▶ Math tools

To do math you need the green **Operator** blocks. Each block does a different problem with the numbers in the two windows.

▼ Placing operators

Wherever you put an **operator** block, it will put the answer to the problem. So if you put it into the window of a **say** block, the cat will say the answer.

Add (+)

The "+" block adds the two numbers in the block together.

Subtract (–)

The "–" block takes the second number away from the first.

Multiply (*)

Scratch uses the "*" symbol, because "**x**" looks like a letter.

Divide (/)

The keyboard has no division sign. Scratch uses "/" instead.

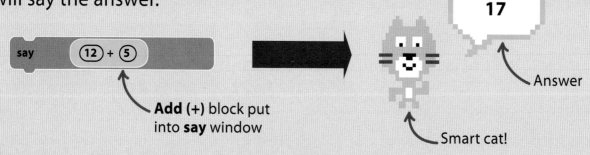

17

Answer

say (12) + (5)

Add (+) block put into **say** window

Smart cat!

▶ Math and variables

We can use **operator** blocks to solve problems with variables. For example, to find the total number of pets, we can use the **add (+)** block to add up the values of the variables **dogs** and **cats**, and store the answer in a variable called **pets**.

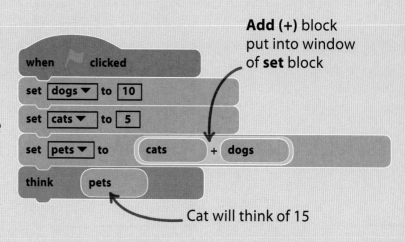

Add (+) block put into window of **set** block

when 🏳 clicked

set dogs ▼ to 10

set cats ▼ to 5

set pets ▼ to (cats + dogs)

think pets

Cat will think of 15

▶ Throwing dice

A random number is one that we can't predict. It's like a number we get when we roll dice—we don't know what the numbers will be before we roll. Scratch can act like dice and "roll" for us. Try this script in a new project.

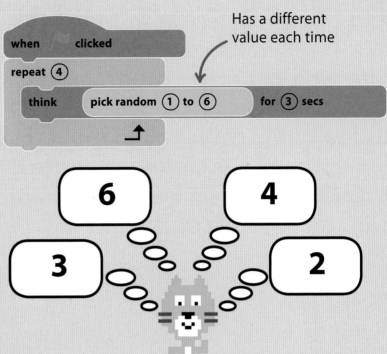

Has a different value each time

Read the script, then run it. The cat will show you four random numbers as it thinks of them. Random numbers are useful in games, because they make the action difficult to guess.

Show what you know
Try these mathematical mind-bogglers.

1. You are the computer! Calculate the values of these blocks.

(3) + (10)   (8) + (11)   (12) – (8)   (22) – (11)   (5) * (6)   (9) / (3)

....

2. These blocks use variables. Can you work out the answers?

set [a ▼] to [10]
set [b ▼] to [2]

(b) + (6)   (a) – (1)   (a) + (b)   (10) * (b)   (b) – (a)   (b) * (a)   (a) / (5)   (a) / (b)

....

3. Write down the values stored in these variables.

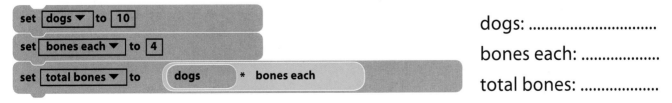

dogs: ....

bones each: ....

total bones: ....

Inputs and events

The data put into a program, such as the answer you type when Scratch asks a question, is called input. Events are actions, like clicking a sprite or pressing a chosen key, that Scratch can use to run scripts.

▼ Just ask

Sprites can use questions and answers using the light blue **ask** and **answer** blocks under the **Sensing** tab. Start a new project and add this script. Read the script. What do you think it does? Run the script to test your ideas.

The cat asks the question

What's for lunch?

You type in "Cat food"

Cat food!

Then press **enter/return** or click the blue check

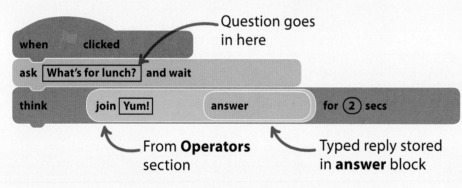

Question goes in here

when clicked

ask | What's for lunch? | and wait

think | join | Yum! | answer | for ② secs

From **Operators** section

Typed reply stored in **answer** block

Lunchtime for Scratch Cat!

The cat asks the question and waits for you to type in your reply using the keyboard. When you press **enter/return**, what you typed in becomes the value of the **answer** block.

Yum! Cat food!

He's always hungry!

Answers are like variables

The **answer** block works just like a variable. Wherever you put the **answer** block it will be replaced by your answer to the question. The green **join** block in the script above just takes what's in its two windows and links them together as a single item.

▶ Events trigger scripts

Events are things that happen that the computer can tell Scratch about, such as key presses and mouse clicks. The brown **Events** "header" blocks start to run a script when a chosen event happens, in the same way that the green flag button can start a script when you click on it.

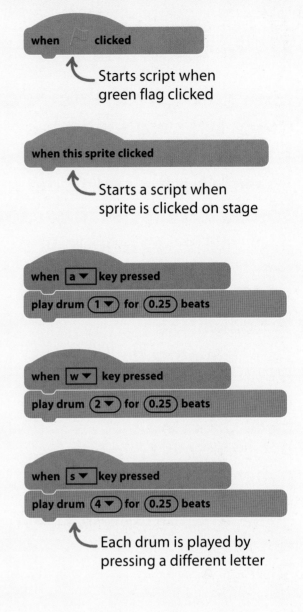

when [flag] clicked

Starts script when green flag clicked

when this sprite clicked

Starts a script when sprite is clicked on stage

▶ Build a drum kit

Create lots of scripts like these. Select a different key and a different drum for each version of the script. The blocks below an **Events** header are run when you press the correct key. Play an epic drum solo using your selected keys!

when [a ▼] key pressed
play drum (1 ▼) for (0.25) beats

when [w ▼] key pressed
play drum (2 ▼) for (0.25) beats

when [s ▼] key pressed
play drum (4 ▼) for (0.25) beats

Each drum is played by pressing a different letter

What a racket!

Show what you know
Can you answer these questions about inputs and events?

1. Which blue **Sensing** block makes a sprite ask a question? ....

2. Which block holds the reply given to the question? ....

3. Something that happens to the computer, like a mouse click or a key press, is called an ....

4. What happens if I click a sprite with this script?

....

....

when this sprite clicked
say [You clicked me!]

5. Can more than one script be running at once? ....

if-then-else

Let's meet the **if-then-else** block. This block uses a question, or **condition**, to choose between two groups of blocks to run. We'll also look at some handy **condition** blocks that use variables and values to ask "true or false?"

What you'll learn:
• How to compare numbers, replies, and variables to make decisions
• How an **if-then-else** block works

▶ Comparing things

There is another kind of block that asks a "true or false?" question. In the green **Operators** section there are 3 blocks that compare what's in their two windows. To read them, you need to know what these symbols mean: =, <, and >.

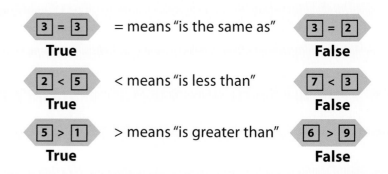

$3 = 3$
True

= means "is the same as"

$3 = 2$
False

$2 < 5$
True

< means "is less than"

$7 < 3$
False

$5 > 1$
True

> means "is greater than"

$6 > 9$
False

We're the same!

We're the same!

▶ Password checker

An **if-then-else** block has two groups of blocks inside. It runs the first group if the condition is true, and the second group if the condition is false. We can use it to check a password.

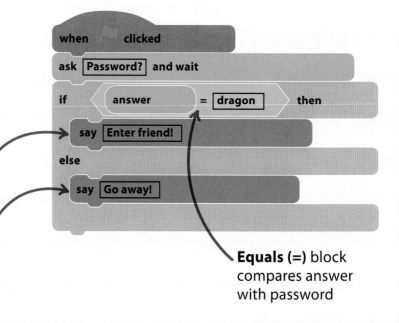

when [ ] clicked

ask `Password?` and wait

if ⟨ answer = `dragon` ⟩ then

say `Enter friend!`

else

say `Go away!`

Block runs if answer is "dragon"

Block runs if answer is NOT "dragon"

Equals (=) block compares answer with password

▶ Friend or foe?

Read and run the script. Only one of the two **say** blocks is run. The other is skipped. We get just one of the replies. If we type in the correct password, the cat greets us. Otherwise ("else"), we're sent away.

If condition is TRUE, then

Enter friend!

else

Go away!

▼ Free ice cream!

The **if-then-else** block can be used to check if you're under 10 and so get some free ice cream. One **say** block gets run, but the other doesn't. Read the script. Run it a few times with different ages.

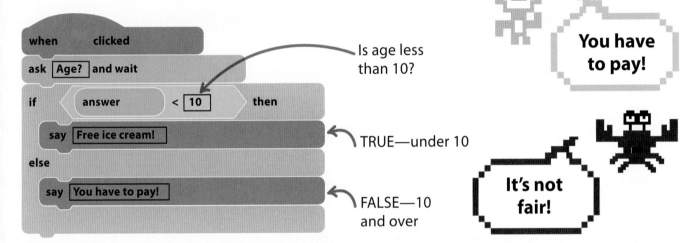

Is age less than 10?

TRUE—under 10

FALSE—10 and over

You have to pay!

It's not fair!

Show what you know
Answer the questions to prove you're a smooth Scratch operator!

1. What shape blocks go into the **condition** window of an **if-then** or **if-then-else** block?

Circle the correct shape

2. Look at the variables below, then circle the green operator blocks that have the value "true."

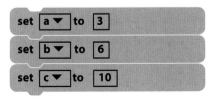

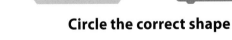

A game: Dragon!

We've learned a lot about Scratch so far. Now let's put it all together into a game. You are the cat. You can control where you are on the stage using the computer mouse. Avoid the ferocious dragon for as long as you can!

What you'll learn:
• How we put a game together from sprites and scripts
• How to detect when two sprites touch
• A script can stop a project

▶ Enter the dragon

Add the "Dragon" sprite to the project. Add a variable for all sprites, and give it the name **speed**.

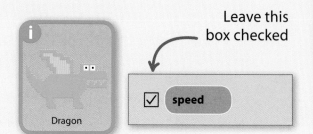

Leave this box checked

Dragon

☑ speed

▶ Get the dragon bouncing

Choose the dragon in the sprite list and add this script. This is the bouncing script we used before, but with a slight change. We control the dragon's speed with a variable and set the dragon off in a different direction in each game. Read and run the script. The dragon bounces around the stage.

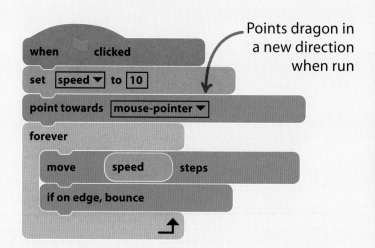

Points dragon in a new direction when run

```
when ⚑ clicked
set speed ▼ to 10
point towards mouse-pointer ▼
forever
    move speed steps
    if on edge, bounce
```

▶ Mouse controls cat!

Now select the cat in the sprite list and add this script. Carefully read the script. It "sticks" the cat to the mouse-pointer. Inside the loop it also checks if we're touching the dragon. If we are, it stops the project—game over! Run the script to check that it works.

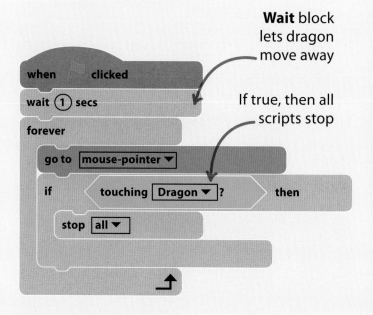

Wait block lets dragon move away

If true, then all scripts stop

```
when ⚑ clicked
wait 1 secs
forever
    go to mouse-pointer ▼
    if touching Dragon ▼ ? then
        stop all ▼
```

▶ Score

A proper game needs a score and a challenge. Add a new variable for all sprites called **score**. Leave it checked so that it shows on the stage.

Add this script to the cat. Read it. For every 3 seconds you avoid the dragon, you score a point. But every time you score, the dragon's speed goes up by one!

Run the game to see that it works as you expect. If it doesn't, check everything from the beginning. Now compete with your friends to get the best score. Why not add a backdrop and some music?

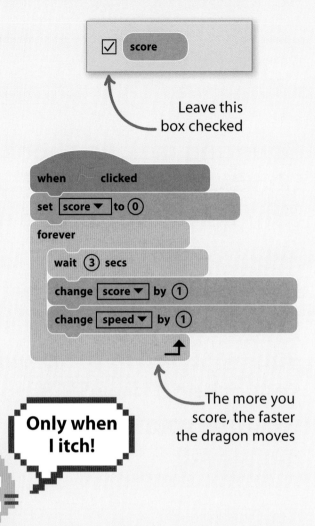

Leave this box checked

The more you score, the faster the dragon moves

Do you like Scratch?

Only when I itch!

Show what you know
Answer the quiz—will it be a high score or "game over?"

1. Why do we leave the check box on the **score** variable checked?

....

2. How could you make the dragon go at half speed at the start?

....

3. Which block could you add inside the cat's **forever** loop to make it look like it's walking? ....

4. How many costumes does the dragon have? ....

5. What would happen if you right-clicked the dragon on the sprite list and chose **duplicate**? ....

....

Games

Bouncing melons, spooky ghosts, and a soccer-playing fish? Let's have fun and make some games!

Reminder boxes will help you remember the skills you mastered in the previous section, and **New Skill boxes** will take your learning to the next level!

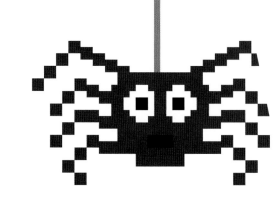

Fishball

Are you ready to build Fishball, your first complicated game? Don't worry, you won't have to do it all at once. Just follow the numbered steps and put the project together piece by piece.

What you'll learn:
• How to build simple scripts to make a game
• How to add sprites, backdrops, and sounds to improve your game
• How to keep track of the time and score

The score and time left in the game are shown here

The fish follows the ball around the stage

Use the green flag and red button to start and stop the game

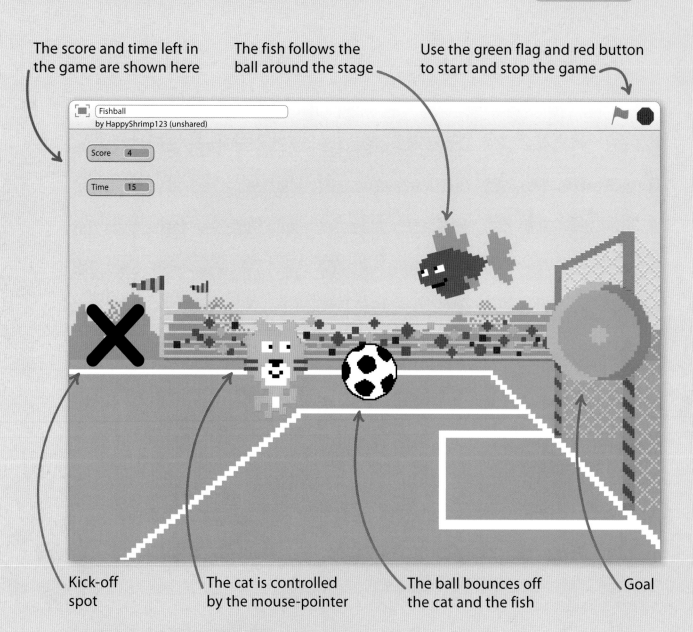

Kick-off spot

The cat is controlled by the mouse-pointer

The ball bounces off the cat and the fish

Goal

▲ Playing the game

Scratch Cat is playing soccer. Use the mouse-pointer to move him around the stage and try to deflect the ball onto the green circle to score a goal. But watch out for the fish goalkeeper—she will do her best to stop you!

Control your cat!

We'll start by creating a simple script to control the cat sprite. It will make the cat stick to the mouse-pointer like glue!

1 Open the Scratch editor: either choose **Create** on the Scratch website or click the Scratch symbol on your computer. Call the project "Fishball."

2 Under the **Scripts** tab, go to the dark blue **Motion** section of the blocks palette. Click on the **go to mouse-pointer** block and drag it to the right into the scripts area.

3 Now click the yellow **Control** section and select the **forever** block. Drag it over the **go to** block, then let go. The two blocks will lock together.

4 Next, choose the brown **Events** section of the blocks palette. Click on the **when green flag clicked** block and add it to the top of the **forever** block. Read the script through. What do you think it does?

Reminder: Forever loops

Loops are sections of code that repeat again and again. A **forever** loop repeats the blocks inside it—forever! In your script to control the cat, the **forever** loop keeps the cat "glued" to the mouse-pointer for the whole game.

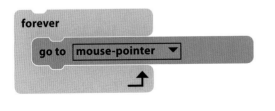

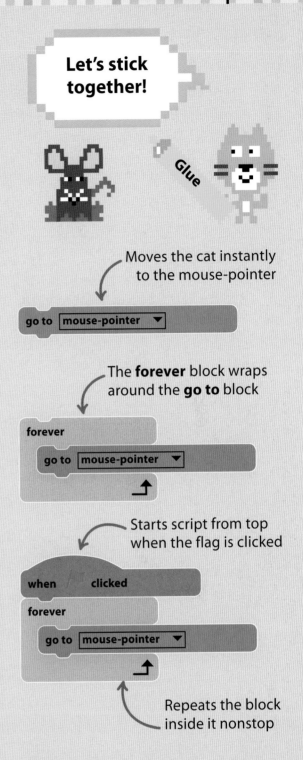

Let's stick together!

Glue

Moves the cat instantly to the mouse-pointer

go to mouse-pointer ▼

The **forever** block wraps around the **go to** block

forever
go to mouse-pointer ▼

Starts script from top when the flag is clicked

when ⚑ clicked
forever
go to mouse-pointer ▼

Repeats the block inside it nonstop

5 Click the green flag at the top of the stage to start (run) the script. The cat should move with the mouse-pointer. If not, check back through steps 1 to 4.

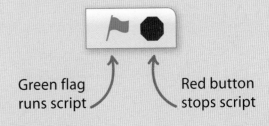

Green flag runs script

Red button stops script

Scratch Cat needs a ball

Now that you can control the cat, it's time to give him a ball to play with. You'll need to create scripts for the ball to make it bounce around the stage and off the cat.

Reminder: Menus and windows

Some blocks have a "drop-down" menu, such as the **point towards** and **touching?** blocks. Click the little triangle to see the options. Then select the one you want.

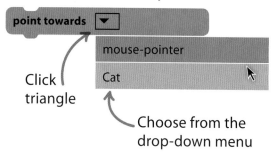

Click triangle

Choose from the drop-down menu

With other blocks, such as **turn arrow degrees**, you click in the window and type in a number.

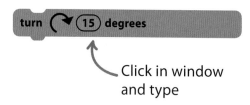

Click in window and type

if-then blocks have a pointed window into which you drag another block that asks a question.

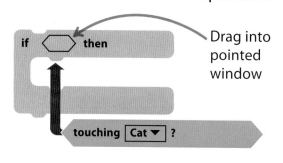

Drag into pointed window

6 Go to the sprite list and click on the **Choose sprite from library** button (the sprite symbol). In the sprite library, select "Soccer Ball" and click **OK**. The ball will appear in the sprite list.

Click the sprite symbol

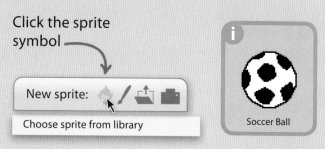

New sprite:

Choose sprite from library

Soccer Ball

7 Next, put these blocks together in the soccer ball's scripts area. Remember that the colour of a block tells you which section you can find it in on the blocks palette.

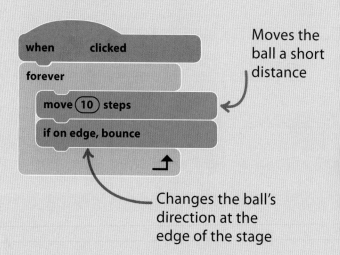

Moves the ball a short distance

Changes the ball's direction at the edge of the stage

8 Click the green flag and watch the ball bounce when it hits the edge of the stage. It won't pay any attention to the cat just yet. The green flag starts the scripts for both the ball and the cat and runs them at the same time.

I'm ignoring the cat!

9 You can make your scripts easier to understand by renaming the cat sprite. In the sprite list (below the stage), select the cat and click on the blue **(i)** in its top corner. Type "Cat" instead of "Sprite1" in the window of the sprite's information panel.

Type "Cat" in this window to change the sprite's name

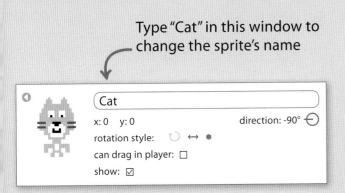

Reminder: if-then

An **if-then** block wraps around other blocks and uses a "true or false?" type question to control when the blocks are run. When Scratch reaches an **if-then** block, it runs the blocks inside only if the answer to the question is true.

Is the ball touching the cat?

True | False

Bounce off Cat ← → Keep going

10 Now select the soccer ball sprite and put together these blocks to add to its script. Place them in the **forever** loop, after the **if on edge, bounce** block. When the ball touches the cat, the script plays a pop sound and makes the ball appear to bounce off the cat.

The **if-then** block checks to see if the ball is touching the cat

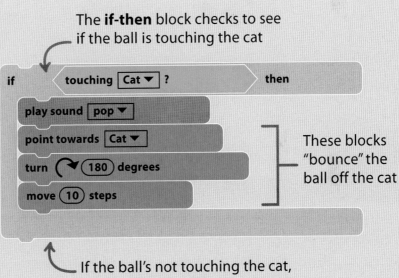

These blocks "bounce" the ball off the cat

If the ball's not touching the cat, the script ignores the instructions inside the **if-then** block

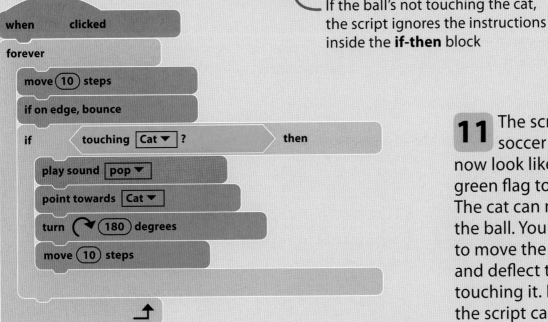

11 The script for the soccer ball should now look like this. Click the green flag to test the script. The cat can now play with the ball. You should be able to move the cat around and deflect the ball by touching it. If not, check the script carefully.

Kicking off, scoring goals

Scratch Cat wants a kick-off spot and a goal to score in. A special kind of block called a **variable** will help you keep track of how many goals are scored during the game.

12 Load two new sprites from the library: "Button1" (the green circle) and "Button5" (the black ×). Drag Button1 to the right of the stage, halfway down, and rename it "Goal." Then drag Button5 to halfway down on the left and rename it "Start."

Fishball
by HappyShrimp123 (unshared)

These two sprites don't need scripts—they're just markers you can send other sprites to

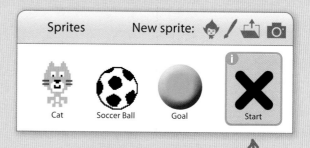

Sprites   New sprite:

Cat   Soccer Ball   Goal   Start

The new sprites will appear in the sprite list

13 In the orange **Data** blocks, click on **Make a Variable**. Type **"Score"** as the variable's name in the pop-up window and hit **OK**. When the block for the variable **Score** appears in the **Data** section, make sure the check box beside it is checked.

Reminder: Variables

A variable is like a labelled box in which you can store data, such as words or numbers. The data stored in a variable is known as its value. The new variable you made has a label, **Score**. It stores the number of goals the cat scores in a game of Fishball. The number of goals is the variable's value.

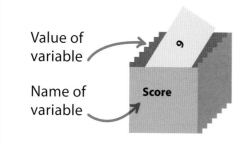

Value of variable

Name of variable

Score

Type in this window

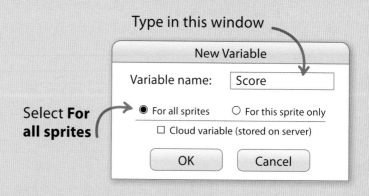

New Variable

Variable name: Score

Select **For all sprites**

● For all sprites   ○ For this sprite only
☐ Cloud variable (stored on server)

OK   Cancel

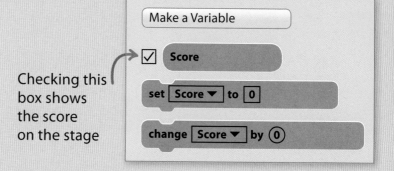

Make a Variable

☑ Score

set Score ▼ to 0

change Score ▼ by 0

Checking this box shows the score on the stage

14 Next, put these two blocks into the soccer ball's script after the **when green flag clicked** block and before the **forever** loop. The orange **set to** block sets the score to zero at the beginning of the game. The dark blue **go to** block sends the ball to the black × ready for the kick-off.

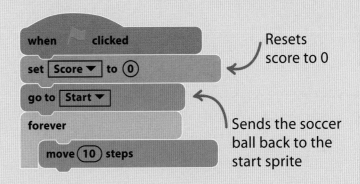

Resets score to 0

Sends the soccer ball back to the start sprite

15 You can add a sound to signal when a goal is scored. Select the soccer ball, go to the **Sounds** tab, and click on **Choose sound from library** (the speaker symbol). In the library, select "rattle" and click **OK** to load it into the project.

Sounds for the sprite can be seen under this tab

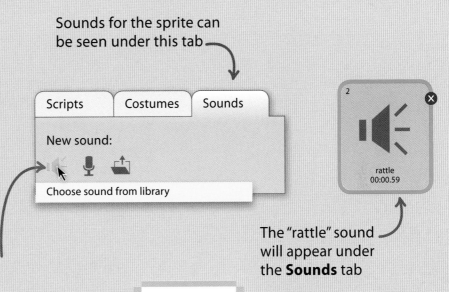

The "rattle" sound will appear under the **Sounds** tab

Click on the speaker symbol to go to the sound library

I prefer tennis!

16 Click on the **Scripts** tab and insert the group of blocks below into the ball's script. Place it under the first **if-then** group, but not inside it. Make sure it is still inside the **forever** loop. You can see the whole script in the next step.

This block, from **Sensing** section, detects when the ball touches the goal

Rattle sound plays each time a goal is scored

The blocks inside the **if-then** block are run only when the ball is touching the goal

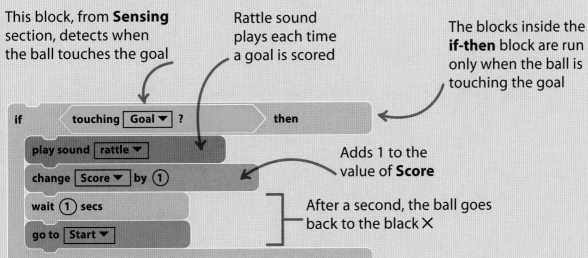

Adds 1 to the value of **Score**

After a second, the ball goes back to the black ×

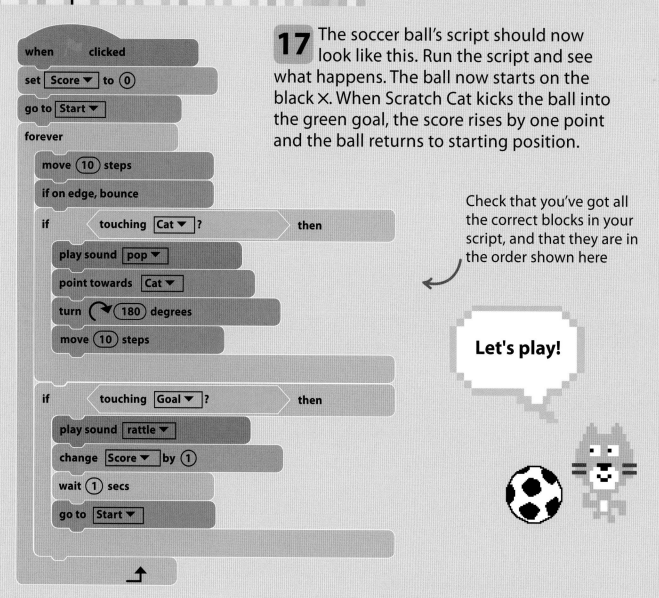

```
when    clicked
set Score ▼ to 0
go to Start ▼
forever
    move 10 steps
    if on edge, bounce
    if         touching Cat ▼ ?         then
        play sound pop ▼
        point towards Cat ▼
        turn ↻ 180 degrees
        move 10 steps

    if         touching Goal ▼ ?         then
        play sound rattle ▼
        change Score ▼ by 1
        wait 1 secs
        go to Start ▼
```

17 The soccer ball's script should now look like this. Run the script and see what happens. The ball now starts on the black X. When Scratch Cat kicks the ball into the green goal, the score rises by one point and the ball returns to starting position.

Check that you've got all the correct blocks in your script, and that they are in the order shown here

Let's play!

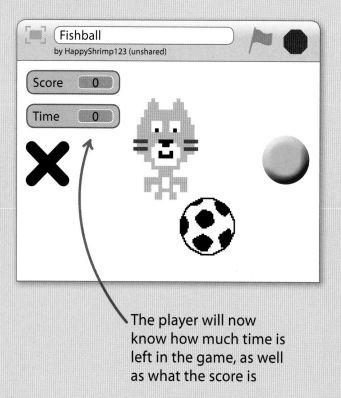

The player will now know how much time is left in the game, as well as what the score is

The pressure's on!

Games are more difficult under pressure. Adding a time limit will make Fishball more challenging. When the green flag is clicked, a 30-second countdown will start.

18 Make a new variable for all sprites called **"Time."** Leave its check box checked so that it shows on the stage.

Make sure this box is checked

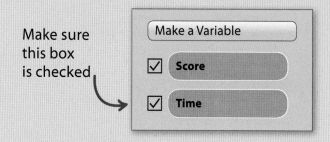

Make a Variable

☑ **Score**

☑ **Time**

19 Add this script to the cat sprite. It will run totally separately from the other script, but at the same time.

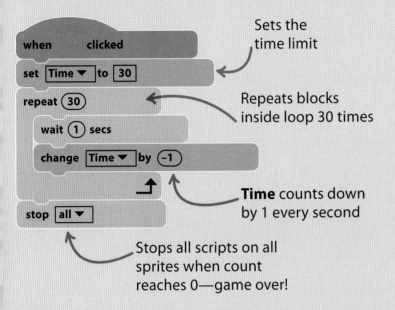

Sets the time limit

Repeats blocks inside loop 30 times

Time counts down by 1 every second

Stops all scripts on all sprites when count reaches 0—game over!

Reminder: Repeat loops

A **repeat loop** repeats the blocks inside it only a fixed number of times, then the next blocks in the script are run. In your time-limit code, the loop takes 1 off the value of **Time** 30 times, then the action moves to the next block (**stop all**).

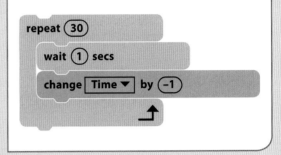

20 Try the game now. How many goals can you score in 30 seconds?

Fishy business

The game's about to get a lot harder! You're going to add a fish goalkeeper to try to stop Scratch Cat from scoring!

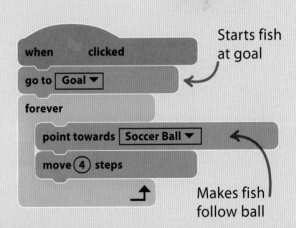

You'll never get past me!

Fish1

21 Go to the sprite library and load "Fish1." Build the script shown on the right in the fish's scripts area. The fish should now always swim slowly toward the ball.

Starts fish at goal

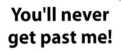

Makes fish follow ball

22 Select the soccer ball. Add this group of blocks to the ball's script to make it bounce off the fish. (It's the same as the code that makes the ball bounce off the cat, but with "Cat" changed to "Fish1" twice.) Put it *between* the two **if-then** blocks, but not inside either of them.

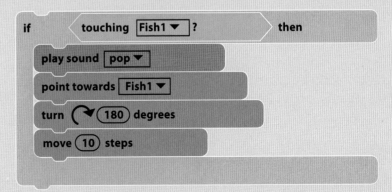

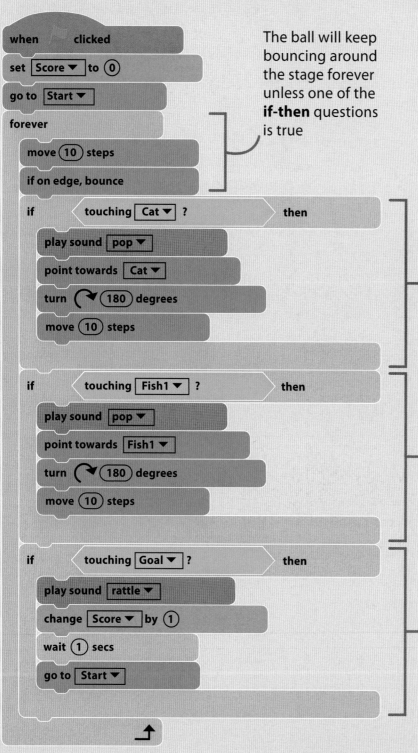

when ⚑ clicked
set Score ▼ to 0
go to Start ▼
forever
  move 10 steps
  if on edge, bounce
  if ⟨ touching Cat ▼ ? ⟩ then
    play sound pop ▼
    point towards Cat ▼
    turn ↻ 180 degrees
    move 10 steps
  if ⟨ touching Fish1 ▼ ? ⟩ then
    play sound pop ▼
    point towards Fish1 ▼
    turn ↻ 180 degrees
    move 10 steps
  if ⟨ touching Goal ▼ ? ⟩ then
    play sound rattle ▼
    change Score ▼ by 1
    wait 1 secs
    go to Start ▼

The ball will keep bouncing around the stage forever unless one of the **if-then** questions is true

If the ball touches the cat, it "bounces" off the cat. It turns around 180 degrees and then moves away from the cat

If the ball touches the fish, it "bounces" off the fish. It turns around 180 degrees and then moves away from the fish

If the ball touches the goal (the green circle), the rattle sound plays and the score goes up by 1. Then the ball goes back to the start (the black ✕)

23 The soccer ball's script is now complete. This is how it should look. Read the script through carefully. Run the script and check that it works as it should.

24 To make Fishball look like a soccer game, click the **Choose backdrop from library** button in the stage info area, at the bottom-left of the screen. Select "goal1," "goal2," or "playing field." Click **OK** to load your chosen backdrop.

Click here to go to backdrop library

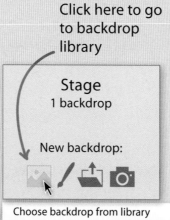

Stage
1 backdrop

New backdrop:
🖼 ✏ ⬆ 📷

Choose backdrop from library

25 Good job—you've made the Fishball Scratch game! Have fun playing it! The skills you've learned while making Fishball will help you to build the other games in this book—and even to invent your own games.

Show what you know
You've aced Fishball, but can you score with this quiz?

1. Label this map of the Scratch editor, using the key below the map. Write one letter for each of the coloured sections.

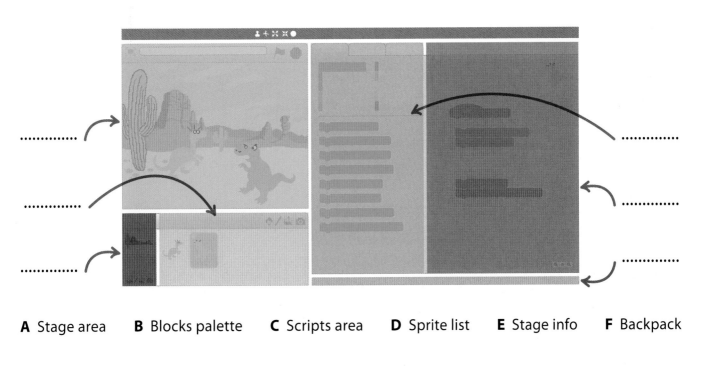

A Stage area   **B** Blocks palette   **C** Scripts area   **D** Sprite list   **E** Stage info   **F** Backpack

2. A .... repeats the blocks inside it nonstop.

3. An .... block either skips or runs the blocks inside it.

4. A .... is a block that stores data.

5. At the moment, the fish moves 4 steps at a time. Would these changes to the fish's **move** block make it swim faster or slower? Circle your answers.

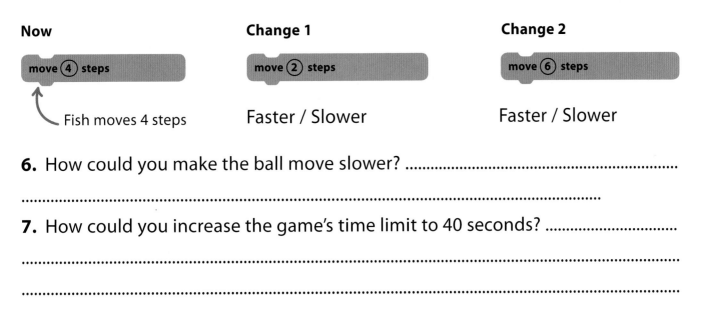

Now

move (4) steps

Fish moves 4 steps

Change 1

move (2) steps

Faster / Slower

Change 2

move (6) steps

Faster / Slower

6. How could you make the ball move slower? ....
....

7. How could you increase the game's time limit to 40 seconds? ....
....
....

Ghost hunt

Things get spooky in this game! You're a witch on a broomstick flying around the city at night in search of friendly ghosts. Ghost Hunt will put your keyboard skills to the test!

What you'll learn:
• How to use keyboard controls to move a sprite
• How coordinates can tell sprites where to go
• That Scratch can use random choices to make games unpredictable

The score and time left in the game are shown here

The ghost glides eerily across the screen

Use the green flag and red button to start and stop the game

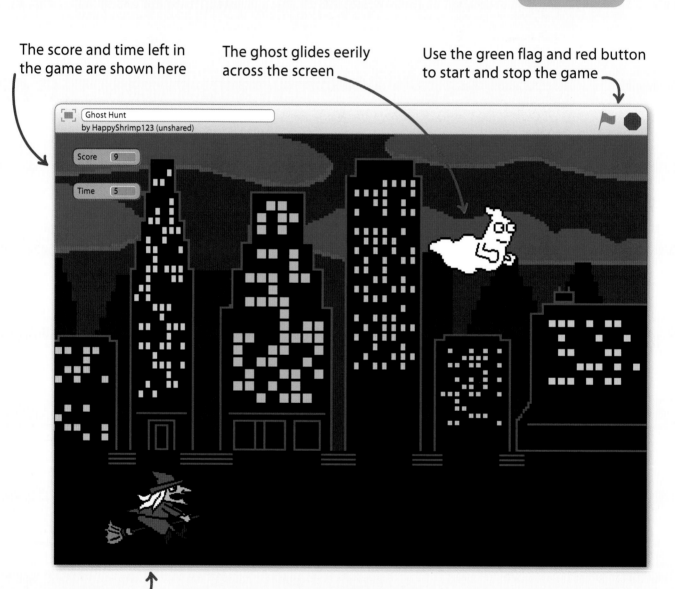

Ghost Hunt
by HappyShrimp123 (unshared)

Score   9

Time   5

You can move the witch anywhere on the screen using the arrow keys on the keyboard

▲ Playing the game

Use the arrow keys to make the witch chase the ghost. When you touch the ghost, it disappears with a pop and you score a point. But the sneaky ghost can reappear anywhere, and it floats randomly around the stage! You have 30 seconds to score as many points as you can.

Good-bye Scratch Cat, hello witch!

The player's sprite for this game will be the witch. You won't need Scratch Cat on the stage, so it's best to delete him.

1 Start a new project. Click on the **File** menu and select **New**. Call the project "Ghost Hunt." As usual, you'll see Scratch Cat on the stage.

2 Go to the sprite list. Right-click on the cat with the computer mouse. Choose **delete** from the pop-up menu.

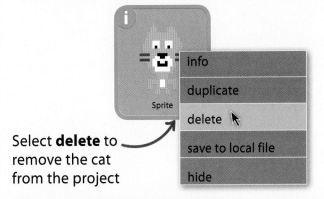

info

duplicate

delete

save to local file

hide

Select **delete** to remove the cat from the project

3 Click on the sprite symbol at the top of the sprite list to go to the library. Select the "Witch" sprite and click **OK** to load her into your game.

Click on the sprite symbol

New sprite:

Choose sprite from library

Witch

New skill: Coordinates

Scratch uses a pair of numbers called x–y coordinates to pinpoint a sprite's position on the stage. The x coordinate tells you where the sprite is across the stage, left or right. The y coordinate shows its up or down position. The coordinates will be positive for right and up, and negative for left and down. In Ghost Hunt, you'll use coordinates to send sprites to different parts of the stage.

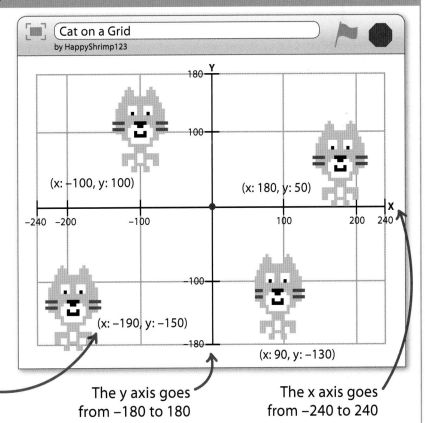

Cat on a Grid
by HappyShrimp123

(x: −100, y: 100)

(x: 180, y: 50)

(x: −190, y: −150)

(x: 90, y: −130)

The x coordinate is always written first

The y axis goes from −180 to 180

The x axis goes from −240 to 240

4 With the witch sprite selected, build this script so that you can use the arrow keys to move her around the stage.

The light blue **Sensing** blocks detect when the arrow keys are pressed

This block moves the witch 10 steps left (−10)

This block moves the witch 10 steps down (−10)

The **forever** loop makes the script check repeatedly for key presses

All the **if-then** blocks must be inside the **forever** loop

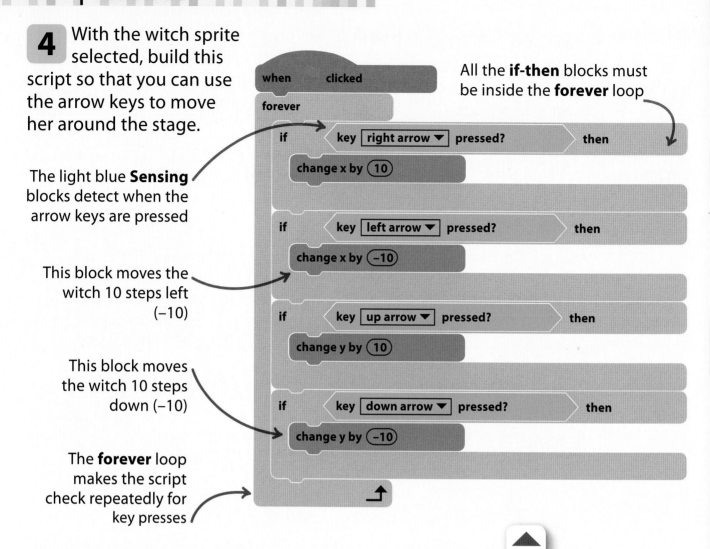

5 Now run the project. You should be able to move the witch all over the stage using the four arrow keys. If it doesn't work, check that you have all the correct blocks and that they are all in the right place.

When an arrow key is pressed, witch moves 10 steps in that direction

A ghost in the city

It's nearly time to introduce the friendly ghost and get it gliding around the stage. But first, add some scenery to make the game look good.

6 Go to the stage info area and click on the first symbol (**Choose backdrop from library**). Select "night city" in the library and hit **OK** to load it into the project.

Click here to open the backdrop library

Click **OK** to load it into the project

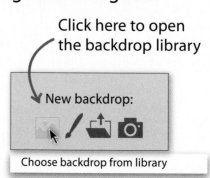

New backdrop:

Choose backdrop from library

night city
480x360

7 Click on the sprite symbol at the top of the sprite list to open the sprite library. Then select "Ghost1" and click **OK** to add it to your project.

Ghost1

8 Next, build the script shown below in Ghost1's script area. This script uses randomly chosen coordinates to make the ghost float unpredictably around the stage. Run the script.

Random numbers

A random number is one you can't guess in advance, like rolling dice. In games, you can use random numbers to make the action difficult to predict.

Makes the ghost appear at the start of the game

Scratch picks random coordinate numbers from within this range

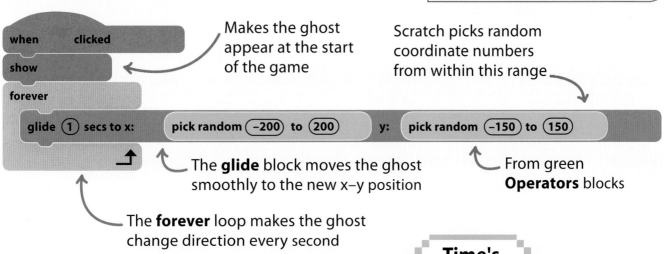

The **glide** block moves the ghost smoothly to the new x–y position

From green **Operators** blocks

The **forever** loop makes the ghost change direction every second

Scoring, timing, and music

At the moment, you have two sprites and a nice backdrop. To turn this project into a game, you need to set up a scoring system and a time limit. Adding some music will help to make the game more fun.

Time's running out!

9 Select the witch, then go to the orange **Data** section. Create two new variables for all sprites and call them **"Score"** and **"Time."** Leave their boxes checked so they show on the stage during the game.

10 Now add this script to the witch sprite. It sets the score to zero at the start of the game. Then it counts down the seconds from 30 and ends the game at 0.

After 30 seconds, this block ends the game

Score always starts from 0

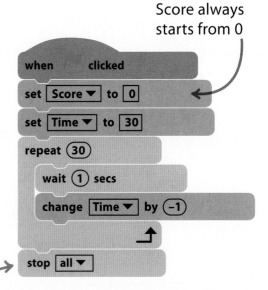

Script waits here
until sprites collide

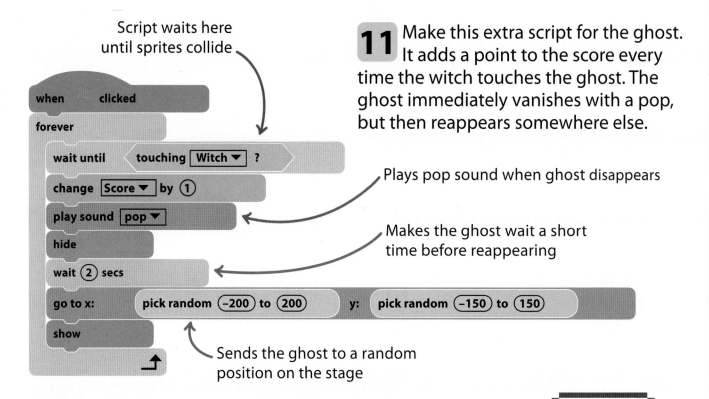

when clicked

forever

> **wait until** ⟨ touching Witch ▼ ? ⟩
>
> **change** Score ▼ **by** ①
>
> **play sound** pop ▼
>
> **hide**
>
> **wait** ② **secs**
>
> **go to x:** ⟨pick random (−200) to (200)⟩ **y:** ⟨pick random (−150) to (150)⟩
>
> **show**

Plays pop sound when ghost disappears

Makes the ghost wait a short
time before reappearing

Sends the ghost to a random
position on the stage

11 Make this extra script for the ghost.
It adds a point to the score every
time the witch touches the ghost. The
ghost immediately vanishes with a pop,
but then reappears somewhere else.

12 Run the game. You'll probably find that the
sprites are so big that they bump into each
other too easily, especially in the middle of the
stage. To help fix this, add these two short scripts.
The first is for the witch, the second is for the ghost.

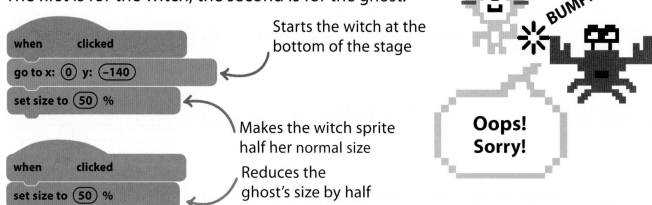

when clicked

go to x: ⓪ **y:** (−140)

set size to (50) **%**

Starts the witch at the
bottom of the stage

when clicked

set size to (50) **%**

Makes the witch sprite
half her normal size

Reduces the
ghost's size by half

13 For the final touch, add some music.
Select the witch sprite, go to the
sound library, and load "dance magic."
Then add this script to loop the music.

when clicked

forever

> **play sound** dance magic ▼ **until done**

The music plays
nonstop while
the game runs

14 Run the game again. You should
find that it's more of a challenge
now. Play it with your friends—who
can catch the most ghosts?

Ouch!

BUMP!

Oops!
Sorry!

It's the
witching
hour!

Show what you know

You're a top ghost hunter, but do these brainteasers spook you?

1. Which order are coordinates written in, (x, y) or (y, x)? ....

2. What are the coordinates of the black x's on this picture of the stage?

A. (_____, _____)   **B.** (_____, _____)   **C.** (_____, _____)   **D.** (_____, _____)

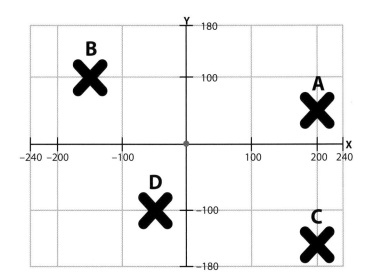

3. Add x's to the stage at these coordinates and label them a, b, c, and d:

a. (100, 0)

b. (0, 50)

c. (−100, −100)

d. (−200, −50)

4. In which direction do these blocks move a sprite: up, down, left, or right?

change x by (100)   change y by (−150)   change y by (50)   change x by (−200)

....

5. Circle the block that moves a sprite smoothly to a particular x–y position.

go to x: (0) y: (0)   glide (1) secs to x: (0) y: (0)   change x by (10)

6a. How would you make the ghost speed up? ....

....

6b. How would you slow down the witch? ....

....

7. Where would you put a **point in direction 90** block and **point in direction −90** block in the witch's main script to make her face the correct way when you press the right and left arrow keys? Try out your ideas.

Rapid reaction

In this game, two players compete to see who has the fastest reaction time. Hit your key with lightning speed to win. If you hesitate for even a fraction of a second, you'll taste defeat!

What you'll learn:
• How to draw sprites and paint backdrops
• How to use the Scratch timer in games
• How to write game instructions and show them on the stage

Player 1's time is shown here

The green circle tells you which player has won

Player 2's time is shown here

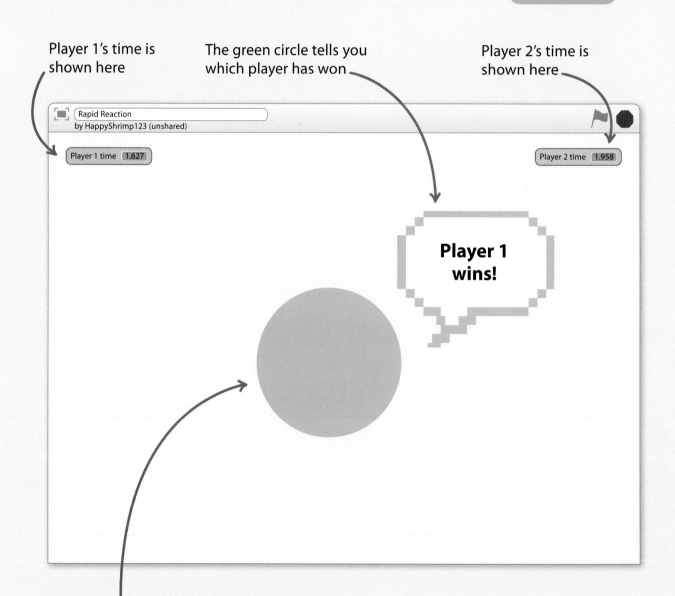

Rapid Reaction
by HappyShrimp123 (unshared)

Player 1 time 1.627

Player 2 time 1.958

Player 1 wins!

Rapid Reaction has only one sprite—a circle that turns from red to green

▲ Playing the game

Clicking the green flag shows the instructions on the stage. Each player has a different key to press: Player 1 the "Z" key, Player 2 the "M" key. When you're ready to play, hit the space bar. Wait until the red circle turns green, then whoever presses fastest wins the game.

Creating the big circle

There's only one sprite in this game. It's a simple coloured circle that you can draw yourself using Scratch's paint editor. The circle starts off red, telling the players to wait before pressing. Then some Scratch magic turns it green to signal "Go!"

Red says "Wait!"

Green says "Go!"

1 Start a new project and name it "Rapid Reaction." Click the paintbrush symbol at the top of the sprite list to open the paint editor.

New sprite:

Click here to paint a new sprite

Circle tool

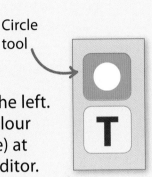

2 Check that **Bitmap Mode** is selected in the bottom-right corner of the paint editor. Then choose red on the colour palette.

3 Click the circle tool on the left. Then select the solid-colour shape (rather than the outline) at the bottom-left of the paint editor.

Select the solid-colour shape

Choose red for the circle colour

Should say **Bitmap Mode** here

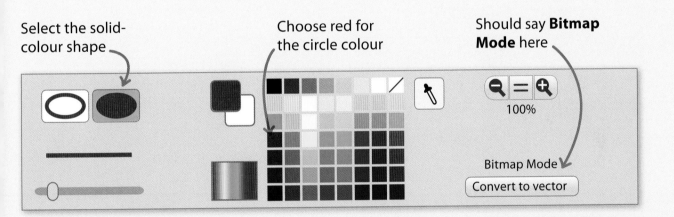

100%

Bitmap Mode

Convert to vector

4 While holding down the shift key, click and drag with the mouse to draw a circle. The circle should be a little bigger than the cat. Click outside the circle. Look at the stage to compare your circle to the cat. When you're happy with the circle's size, drag it to the centre of the stage. Then right-click on the cat and select delete.

See you later!

New skill: Resizing the circle

You can use the **Shrink** and **Grow** tools at the top of the Scratch screen to make your circle smaller or bigger. Click on the tool and then on the thing you want to shrink or grow.

Shrink

Grow

Scripts for the sprites

You'll build most of the code for Rapid Reaction in the scripts area of the circle sprite. This game uses Scratch's built-in timer. You can find blocks for the timer in the light blue **Sensing** section.

5 In the **Data** section of the **Scripts** tab, make three variables for all sprites: **"Player 1 time," "Player 2 time,"** and **"Presses."** Uncheck the check box for **Presses**.

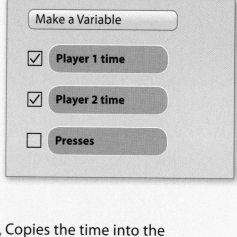

6 Add this script to the circle sprite. After hitting the space bar, it records how long Player 1 takes to hit the "Z" key. It also checks to see if Player 1 reacts first.

Pressing "Z" runs the rest of the script

Copies the time into the **Player 1 time** variable, then shows it on the stage

Adds 1 to **Presses** variable, which counts the number of key presses

If "Z" is the first key pressed, the script says Player 1 is the winner

Reminder: Comparison operators

In the **Operators** section are three green blocks that compare what's in their two windows. You can use a **comparison operator** in an **if-then** block to decide when the blocks inside it are run.

2 < 5   is less than

3 = 3   equals

5 > 1   is more than

7 Now build the script below to record Player 2's reaction. It's almost the same as the last script, except that it's triggered by the "M" key and it uses the **Player 2 time** variable.

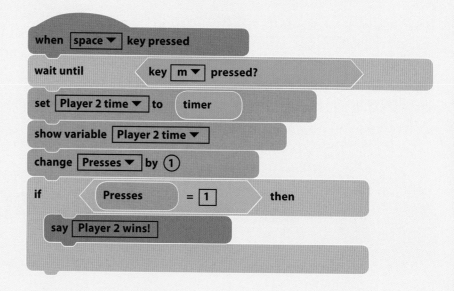

Script waits between 3 and 6 seconds after space key is pressed before changing the circle's colour

8 This new script makes the red circle turn green to tell the players to press their keys. It lets the timer run until both players have pressed. If their reaction times are the same, it's a draw.

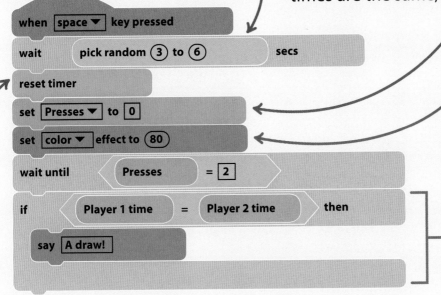

This block sets the key-press counter to 0

This smart block from the purple **Looks** section changes the red circle to green

Resets timer to 0 when the circle changes colour

If both players press at the same time, the circle sprite declares the game a draw

9 Make this last script for the circle. It hides the players' time displays and resets the circle's colour to red at the beginning. Click the green flag, then the space bar to start the game. Does it work OK? If it doesn't, check your code.

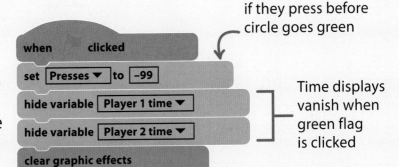

This block stops players from winning if they press before circle goes green

Time displays vanish when green flag is clicked

Cancels the **set color effect to 80** block

Instructions

So that the players know the rules of Rapid Reaction, you can create a special sprite that shows the instructions when the game begins.

Click on the big **"T"**

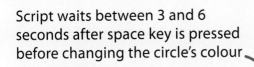

How do I play this game?

10 Your instructions sprite will just be text on a see-through background. Use the paintbrush symbol to create a new blank sprite and call it "Instructions." Make sure you are in **Bitmap Mode** in the paint editor. Then select the text tool on the left.

11 Choose black from the palette as the colour for the text. Click on the checkered drawing area and type out the instructions shown on the right.

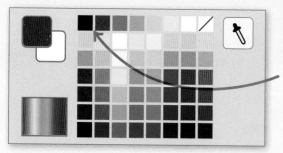

Select black for the text colour

Who has the quickest reactions?

When circle goes green:
Player 1 press Z
Player 2 press M

Press space bar to start.

12 You can change the look of the type at this stage by clicking on **Font** at the bottom-left of the paint editor. There are six fonts to choose from. If the text doesn't fit, use the **Select** tool (the hand symbol) to resize it. Drag a box around the text and pull the corner points of the text box in or out. When you're finished, click outside the box to stop editing.

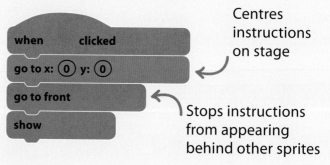

Select tool

Use the corner points to resize the block

13 Give the instructions sprite these scripts. They show the instructions at the start of the game, then hide them when the space bar is pressed. Run the game to check that the scripts work.

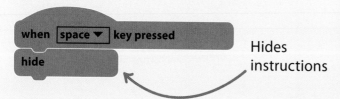

Hides instructions

Centres instructions on stage

Stops instructions from appearing behind other sprites

14 Now go to the stage. Click on the **Player 2 time** window. Drag it into the top-right corner. This will help each player to see their time clearly.

15 Lastly, add a coloured backdrop. To open the paint editor, click the paintbrush in the stage info area (bottom-left of the screen). Pick a colour, select the **Fill with color** tool (the paint pot), and click on the drawing area. That's it—you're ready to play Rapid Reaction!

Fill with color tool

Paint new backdrop

New backdrop:

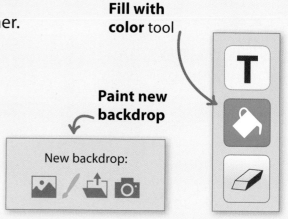

Show what you know
How will you react when you tackle these fiendish questions?

1. You can resize sprites using the .... and .... tools above the stage, at the top of the Scratch screen.

2. Which of these tools will you NOT find in the Scratch paint editor? Mark your answer.

● ....　　　T ....

⬦ ....　　　✂ ....

3. In which section will you find the **timer** block? ....

4. True or false: unchecking a variable's check box will make it appear on the stage. ....

5. Which coordinates centre a sprite on the stage? Circle your answer.

go to x: (240) y: (180)　　　go to x: (100) y: (−180)　　　go to x: (0) y: (0)

6. Try putting these numbers into the window of the **set color effect to** block. What colours do you get when the red circle changes?

20 ....　　　30 ....　　　100 ....

130 ....　　　150 ....　　　180 ....

7. What do these three comparison operator blocks mean?

a > b　　　c < d　　　d = e

a .... b　　　c .... d　　　d .... e

8. To make the game more fun, you can add sounds that play when the players press their keys. Where would you put these two blocks in the players' scripts? Try out your ideas in Scratch.

Player 1

play sound [duck ▼]

Player 2

play sound [goose ▼]

Melon bounce

Scratch Cat has to stop the falling watermelons from hitting the ground, but he doesn't know where they'll appear or which melon will drop first! Help him to keep the melons in the air.

Each melon starts in a random position

The melons bounce off the cat and back up into the air

The melons fall one by one

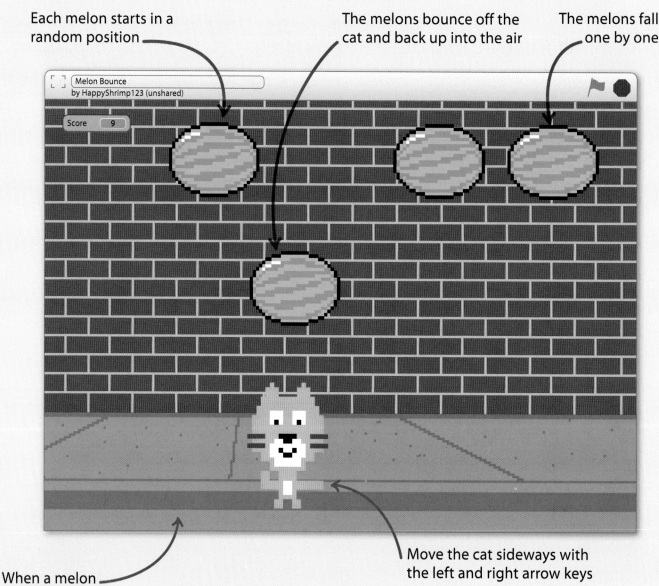

Move the cat sideways with the left and right arrow keys

When a melon hits the bottom of the stage, you hear a cymbal and it's the end of the game

▲ Playing the game

Use the arrow keys to move Scratch Cat back and forth across the stage to reach the falling melons. You get a point for every second the game lasts. The longer you keep the melons bouncing, the more points you score!

Getting the cat moving

First, make some code so that Scratch Cat can patrol along the bottom of the stage, keeping the watermelons off the ground.

1 Start a new project and name it "Melon Bounce." Change the cat's name from "Sprite1" to "Cat."

2 Look under the cat's **Costumes** tab. You'll see he has two costumes. If you make him switch costumes repeatedly, it will look like he is walking. This is called animation.

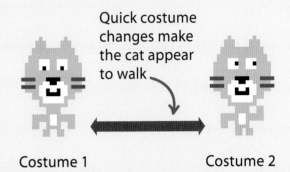

Quick costume changes make the cat appear to walk

Costume 1   Costume 2

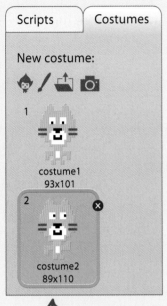

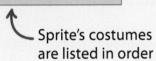

Sprite's costumes are listed in order

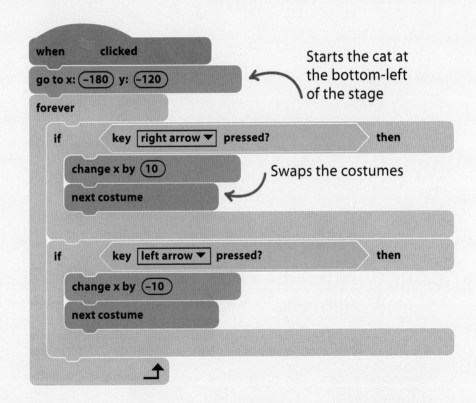

Starts the cat at the bottom-left of the stage

Swaps the costumes

3 Create this script so that you can move the cat along the bottom of the stage using the left and right arrow keys. The purple **next costume** blocks change the cat's costume every 10 steps.

Multiple melons

To make the four melons, you'll load one sprite, give it one script, and then make three copies of it.

4 In the sprite list, click on the sprite symbol (**Choose sprite from library**). Load the "Watermelon" sprite.

Watermelon

5 Add a sound for when the melon hits the ground. Under the watermelon's **Sounds** tab, click on the speaker symbol (**Choose sound from library**). Load the "cymbal" sound.

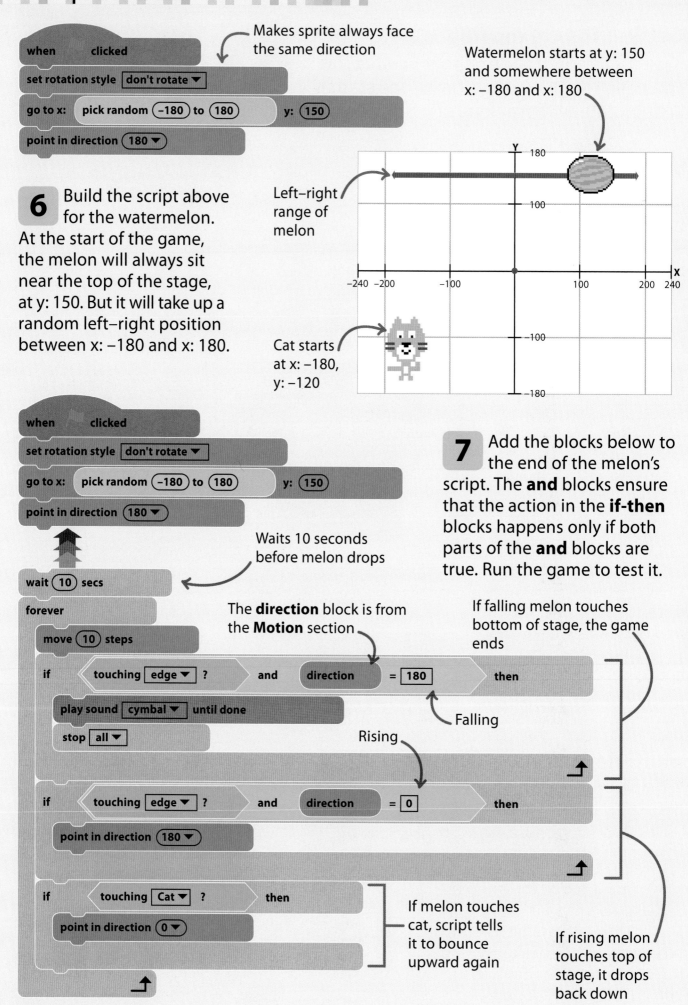

Makes sprite always face the same direction

when clicked
set rotation style don't rotate ▼
go to x: pick random (–180) to (180) y: (150)
point in direction (180 ▼)

Watermelon starts at y: 150 and somewhere between x: –180 and x: 180

6 Build the script above for the watermelon. At the start of the game, the melon will always sit near the top of the stage, at y: 150. But it will take up a random left–right position between x: –180 and x: 180.

Left–right range of melon

Cat starts at x: –180, y: –120

when clicked
set rotation style don't rotate ▼
go to x: pick random (–180) to (180) y: (150)
point in direction (180 ▼)

7 Add the blocks below to the end of the melon's script. The **and** blocks ensure that the action in the **if-then** blocks happens only if both parts of the **and** blocks are true. Run the game to test it.

Waits 10 seconds before melon drops

wait (10) secs
forever
move (10) steps

The **direction** block is from the **Motion** section

If falling melon touches bottom of stage, the game ends

if touching edge ▼ ? and direction = 180 then
play sound cymbal ▼ until done
stop all ▼

Falling

Rising

if touching edge ▼ ? and direction = 0 then
point in direction (180 ▼)

if touching Cat ▼ ? then
point in direction (0 ▼)

If melon touches cat, script tells it to bounce upward again

If rising melon touches top of stage, it drops back down

8 To make the game trickier, add three more melons. Copy the watermelon and its code by right-clicking on it and selecting **duplicate** from the pop-up menu. Do this two more times, so you have four melons.

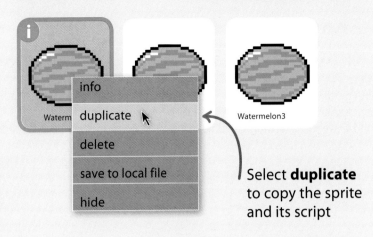

Select **duplicate** to copy the sprite and its script

9 Change the **wait 10 secs** block in the scripts of the three duplicate melons so that the melons all drop at different times. Alter their waiting times to 15, 20, and 25 seconds.

Watermelon2
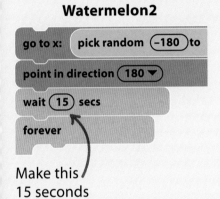

Make this 15 seconds

Watermelon3
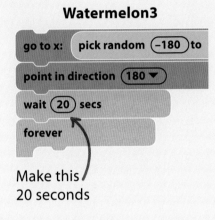

Make this 20 seconds

Watermelon4
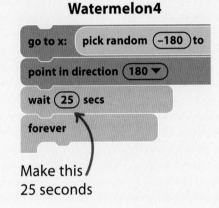

Make this 25 seconds

Scoring and scenery

You've nearly finished building Melon Bounce. All that's left to do is to create a script to keep score and to add some scenery to the stage.

What a waste of melons!

10 Make a new variable for all sprites called **"Score."** Leave its check box checked. Add this script to the cat. It adds 1 to the score for every second that the game lasts.

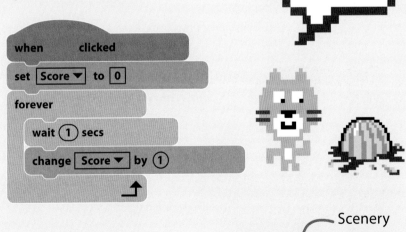

11 Go to the stage info area and click on the first symbol (**Choose backdrop from library**). Select "brick wall1" in the library and hit **OK**. The game's now complete. Keep those melons in the air!

Click here

New backdrop:

Choose backdrop from library

Scenery appears under the stage's **Backdrops** tab

brick wall1 480x360

Show what you know

Now that you've mastered the melons, try these mind-bogglers.

1. What colour are the blocks in these sections of the blocks palette?

Data ....   Sound ....

Events ....   Sensing ....

Motion ....   Control ....

Operators...   Looks..

2. Quickly switching a sprite's costumes to make it look as if it's walking or running is called ....

3. Would making the cat move faster make the game easier or harder?...................................

4. How could you make the melons fall faster? ....
....

5. How could you make the melons smaller?..
....

6. How could you add more melons to the game?..
....

7. The melons occasionally bunch together at the start, which makes the game far too easy. You can fix this by changing the **pick random** range in the **go to x** blocks of the melon's scripts, as shown below. Try it yourself.

Watermelon

pick random 40 to 180

Watermelon2

pick random 40 to 180

Watermelon3

pick random -180 to -40

Watermelon4

pick random -180 to -40

How does this solve the bunching problem? ....
....
....

8. Try building a short script to play music while the game is running. Add it to the cat sprite. Test your script.

Melons!
Melons!
Melons!

Projects

Now that you're a Scratch expert, let's see what you can do! Use your skills to make weird music, wacky art, and a tricky quiz to challenge your friends.

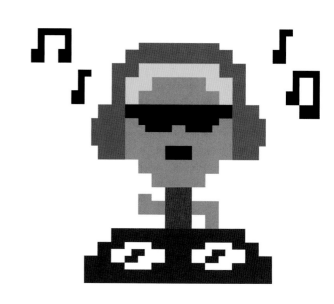

Weird music

Are you ready to build **Weird Music**, and amaze your friends and family with your compositions? Follow the numbered steps and put the project together piece by piece.

What you'll learn:
• How to build simple scripts to make a project
• How to control a sprite
• How to play music in Scratch
• How to make sprites change size and colour

This readout shows the direction from the cat to the mouse-pointer

Type the name of your project here

Notes change according to where the mouse-pointer is on the stage

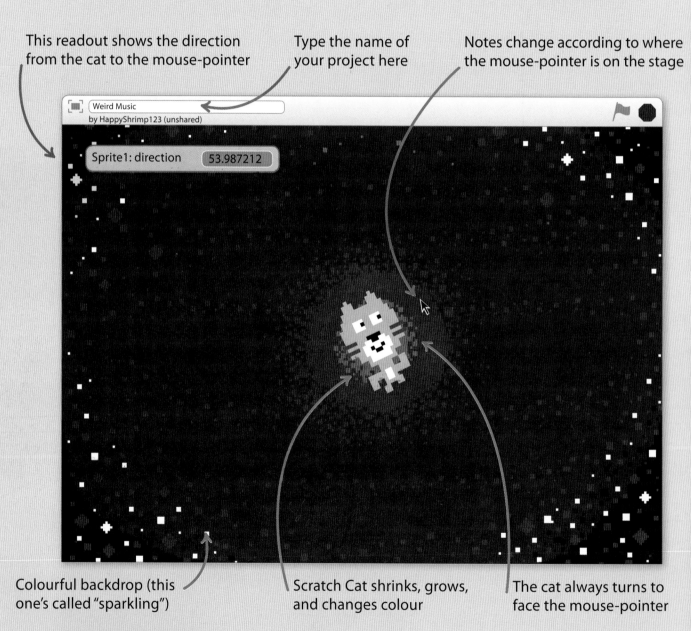

Colourful backdrop (this one's called "sparkling")

Scratch Cat shrinks, grows, and changes colour

The cat always turns to face the mouse-pointer

▲ What you do

This project turns the stage into a strange musical instrument. Click with the mouse to play a note. Click on a different part of the stage and the note changes. All the while, Scratch Cat spins around in the centre, changing colour and size!

Get Scratch Cat spinning!

First, we'll make a script to control the cat. He'll remain in the centre of the stage, but he won't stay still!

I'm getting dizzy!

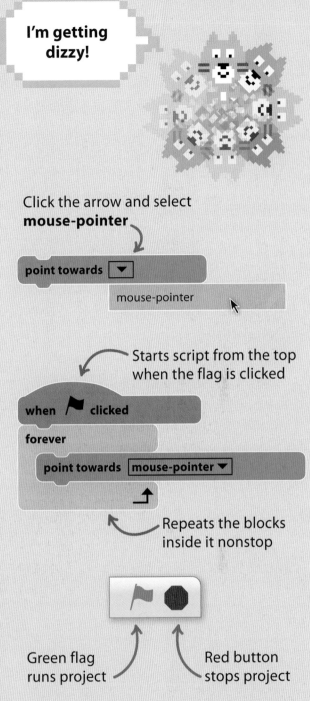

1 Open the Scratch editor: either choose **Create** on the Scratch website or click the Scratch symbol on your computer. Call your project "Weird Music."

Click the arrow and select **mouse-pointer**

point towards ▼
mouse-pointer

2 Under the **Scripts** tab, look at the dark blue **Motion** section of the blocks palette. Click on the **point towards** block and drag it to the right into the scripts area. Select **mouse-pointer** from the drop-down menu.

Starts script from the top when the flag is clicked

when 🏴 clicked
forever
point towards mouse-pointer ▼

3 Click the yellow **Control** section and select the **forever** block. Drag it over the **point towards** block, then let go. The blocks will lock together. Next, click the brown **Events** section. Drag the **when flag clicked** block to the top of the **forever** block.

Repeats the blocks inside it nonstop

4 Click the green flag at the top of the stage to start (run) the project. The cat should rotate so that he always faces the mouse-pointer. If he doesn't, check your script.

Green flag runs project

Red button stops project

Reminder: "forever" loops

Loops are sections of code that repeat again and again. A **forever** loop repeats the blocks inside it—forever! In your script to control the cat, the **forever** loop keeps the cat pointing at the mouse-pointer.

forever
point towards mouse-pointer ▼

5 Now go back to the **Motion** section. Click the small box next to the **direction** block. This will show the direction in which the cat is pointing on the stage.

Check this box to show the direction on the stage

☐ x position
☐ y position
☑ direction

Play a note

Next, we'll build a second script for Scratch Cat. This script will allow us to play notes on musical instruments.

Click here to see the drop-down instrument list

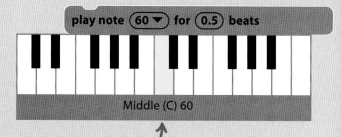

set instrument to 1 ▼

| (1) Piano |
| (2) Electric piano |
| (3) Organ |
| (4) Guitar |
| (5) Electric guitar |
| (6) Bass |

The list goes on: there are 21 instruments to choose from in all

6 Go to the pink **Sound** section and drag the **set instrument to** block into the cat's scripts area. This will be the first block of your second script. The arrow in the block's window lets you choose different instruments. Leave it set to **1** (the piano) for now.

7 Add this pink **play note** block from the **Sound** section to the bottom of the **set instrument to** block. It lets you choose which note to play and for how long. Keep it set to **note 60** and **0.5 beats**.

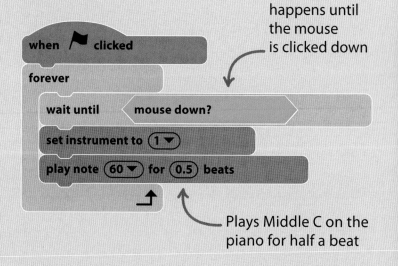

play note 60 ▼ for 0.5 beats

Middle (C) 60

Note 60 plays "Middle C"—the note in the centre of a piano keyboard

8 Use your two pink blocks to build the second script shown here. You'll find the **wait until** block and the **forever** loop in the yellow **Control** section. The **mouse down?** block is in the light blue **Sensing** section.

when 🏳 clicked

forever

wait until   mouse down?

set instrument to 1 ▼

play note 60 ▼ for 0.5 beats

Nothing happens until the mouse is clicked down

Plays Middle C on the piano for half a beat

Who ever heard of a cat playing the piano?

9 Click the green flag to run the project. The piano should play a note when you click down with the mouse. If it doesn't, check that your script is correct. Experiment by playing different notes of different lengths, and see what other instruments sound like.

Make some music

Let's tweak the main script. The notes you play and their loudness (volume) will be controlled by the distance and direction from the cat to the mouse-pointer.

10 To understand how directions work on the stage, look at the picture below. Scratch describes the direction in which a sprite is facing in degrees (°), so our turtle is facing right (90°).

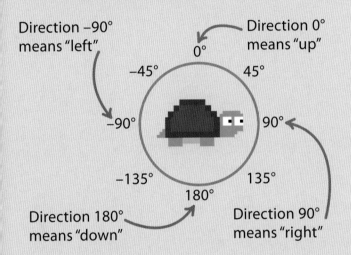

Direction –90° means "left"

Direction 0° means "up"

Direction 180° means "down"

Direction 90° means "right"

Reminder: Arithmetic operators

Four blocks in the green **Operators** section can do math with whatever numbers you type into them. You can also put variables and other blocks in their windows to do calculations.

Add (+)   Subtract (−)

Multiply (×)   Divide (÷)

You can put one **arithmetic operator** inside another to do more difficult calculations.

Inner block is worked out first

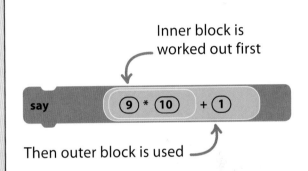

Then outer block is used

11 Stack these blocks in the left-hand window of the **play note** block. The **direction** block goes into the **divide operator**, which itself slots into the **add operator**.

We put new instructions in the **play note** window

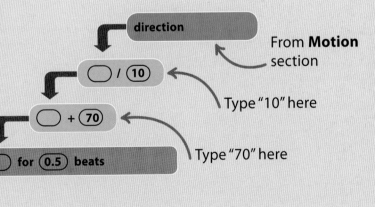

From **Motion** section

Type "10" here

Type "70" here

12 Replace the **set instrument to** block in your script with a pink **set volume to** block. Stack these two blocks into its window, as shown here.

This block replaces the **set instrument to** block

Select **mouse-pointer**

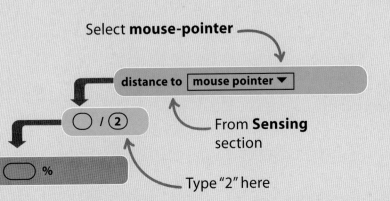

From **Sensing** section

Type "2" here

13 Your script should now look like this. Run the project. The notes you play will change as you move the mouse-pointer around the stage. They will also get louder farther away from the cat.

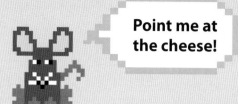

Point me at the cheese!

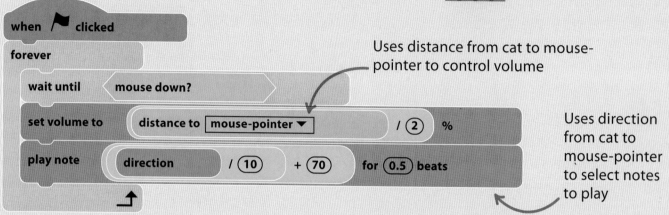

Uses distance from cat to mouse-pointer to control volume

Uses direction from cat to mouse-pointer to select notes to play

Finishing touches

Our final code tweaks will make Scratch Cat turn all the colours of the rainbow and shrink or grow in size as you play your crazy tunes.

14 Put the two blocks below into the **forever** loop, between the pink blocks. The **set size to** block enlarges or shrinks the cat as the volume changes. The **set color effect to** block changes his colour as the mouse-pointer moves around the stage. Run the project and check that it works.

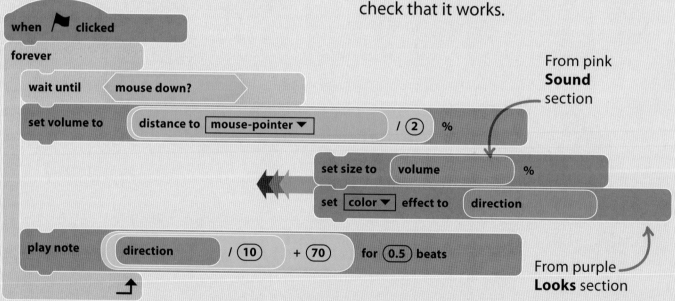

From pink **Sound** section

From purple **Looks** section

15 Finally, add a colourful backdrop. Click on the **Choose backdrop from library** symbol in the stage info area, at the bottom-left of the Scratch editor. In the library, select "sparkling" or another backdrop. Click **OK** to load it into the project. You're done! It's time to start composing!

Click on this symbol

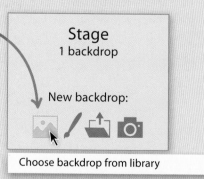

Stage
1 backdrop

New backdrop:

Choose backdrop from library

Show what you know

You can make music, but can you make sense of these questions?

1. What colour are the **Looks** blocks? ....

2. A .... repeats the blocks inside it endlessly.

3. Can you calculate the value of each block?

a. ⟨17 + 2⟩   **b.** ⟨9 - 4⟩   **c.** ⟨3 * 4⟩   **d.** ⟨15 / 3⟩

e. ⟨⟨8 + 2⟩ * 3⟩   **f.** ⟨3 + ⟨8 * 2⟩⟩

a. .... **b.** .... **c.** .... **d.** ....

e. .... **f.** ....

4. Draw a line from each turtle to the correct direction value.

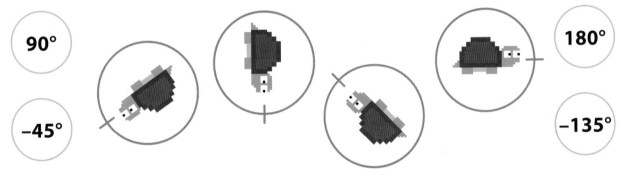

5. Run the project and hold down the mouse button. What happens?

....

6. Go to the pink **Sound** blocks. Check the box beside the **volume** block.

What happens? ....

Check this box ↘ ☑ volume

7. Can you figure out what this script does? Try adding it to the cat and

pressing the space bar as you play. ....

....

```
when space ▼ key pressed
set instrument to    pick random 1 to 21
```

Skywriting

In Skywriting, you'll use Scratch's **stamp** block, from the dark green **Pen** section, to spray patterns, messages, and pictures onto the stage. You can even make your own firework display!

What you'll learn:
• What variables are
• How **if-then** blocks work
• How to use the **stamp** and **clear** blocks
• How to make and use sliders for variables

Move this slider to make the spray broad or narrow

Low values on the **Width** slider narrow the spray so you can draw lines

Move this slider to change the colour of the splotches

High values on the **Width** slider spray the splotches over a wider area

Starry-sky backdrop

▲ What you do

Click down with the mouse to spray splotches of colour onto the stage. Move the sliders to change the spray's spread and colour. Hit the "c" key to clear the stage and start again.

Make a splotch!

The only sprite we need is a ball. We'll shrink it so that it looks like a tiny splotch of colour. Then we can use it to create all sorts of shapes and patterns on the stage, and even to write.

See you later!

1 Start a new project. Call it "Skywriting." In the sprite list, right-click on the cat. Select **delete** from the pop-up menu. Good-bye, Scratch Cat!

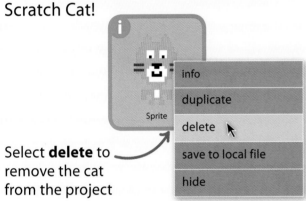

Select **delete** to remove the cat from the project

2 Click on the sprite symbol at the top of the sprite list to go to the library. Choose the "Ball" sprite and click **OK** to load it into your game.

Click the sprite symbol

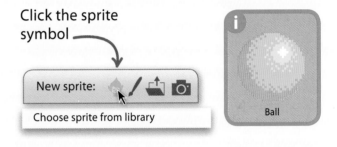

Choose sprite from library

Ball

3 Next, build and run this script. Clicking the mouse "stamps" a splotch (a tiny image of the Ball sprite) onto the stage. Keep the mouse button pressed down to draw lines.

Change the number here from 100 to 10

Blocks inside run only when mouse button is pressed

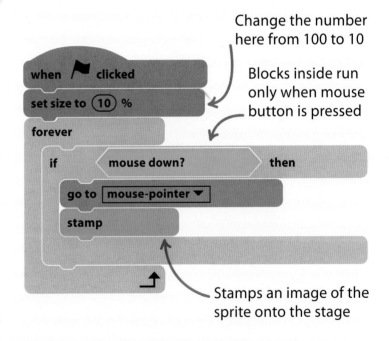

Stamps an image of the sprite onto the stage

4 Now make the short script below. It erases all the splotches when you press "c."

Reminder: "if-then"

An **if-then** block wraps around other blocks and uses a "true or false?" question to control whether those blocks are run or skipped. When Scratch gets to an **if-then** block, it runs the blocks inside only if the answer to the question is true.

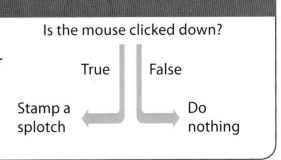

Is the mouse clicked down?

True / False

Stamp a splotch / Do nothing

5 In the orange **Data** section, click on **Make a Variable**. Type **"Width"** as the variable's name in the pop-up window and hit **OK**. When the block for the variable **Width** appears in the **Data** section, make sure the check box beside it is checked so it can be seen on the stage.

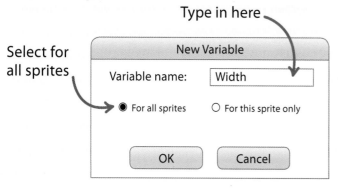

Type in here

Select for all sprites

New Variable

Variable name: Width

● For all sprites   ○ For this sprite only

OK   Cancel

Reminder: Variables

A variable is like a labelled box in which you can store data, such as words or numbers. The data stored in a variable is called its value. The variable you made has the label **Width**. The value it stores is the width of the splotch spray, measured in steps across the stage.

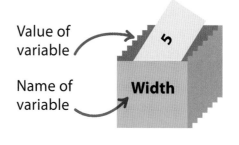

Value of variable

Name of variable

Width

A check in this box shows the variable on the stage

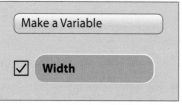

Make a Variable

☑ **Width**

Draw a picture of me!

Spray some colour

It's time to create the spray effect. We can do this by making a few changes to the tiny Ball sprite's main script.

6 Add these blocks to the ball's main script. Put the **set Width to** block outside the forever loop. Click the flag to try out the spray effect.

Type "5" into this window to set the width of the spray

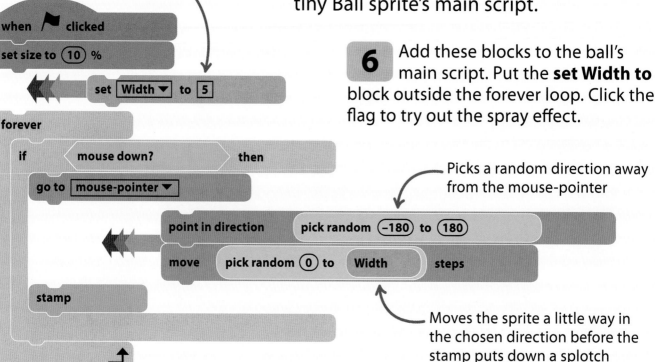

```
when ⚑ clicked

set size to 10 %

set Width ▼ to 5

forever
    if   mouse down?   then
        go to mouse-pointer ▼

        point in direction   pick random -180 to 180

        move   pick random 0 to Width   steps

        stamp
```

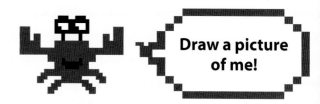

Picks a random direction away from the mouse-pointer

Moves the sprite a little way in the chosen direction before the stamp puts down a splotch

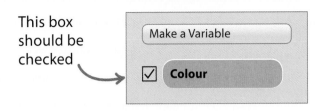

7 Create a new variable called **"Colour."** Make sure its check box is checked so the variable appears on the stage.

This box should be checked

Make a Variable

☑ **Colour**

8 Add this block to the main script. It sets the colour of the splotches to whatever you select with the **Colour** slider. (We'll make the slider next.)

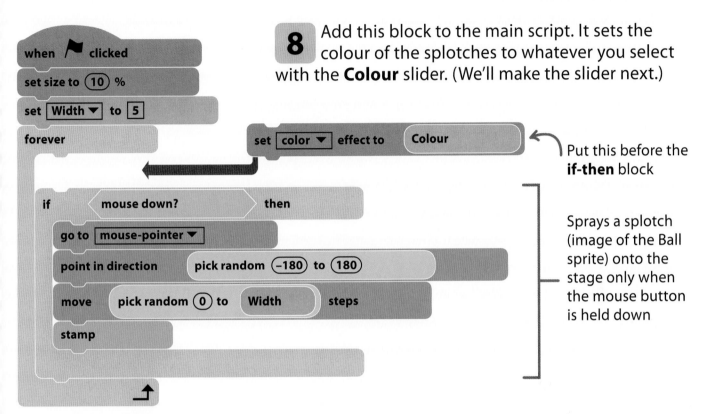

when ⚑ clicked

set size to (10) %

set [Width ▼] to [5]

forever

set [color ▼] effect to (Colour)

Put this before the **if-then** block

if ⟨ mouse down? ⟩ then

go to [mouse-pointer ▼]

point in direction (pick random (-180) to (180))

move (pick random (0) to (Width)) steps

stamp

Sprays a splotch (image of the Ball sprite) onto the stage only when the mouse button is held down

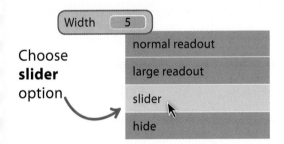

Width   5

normal readout

large readout

slider

hide

Choose **slider** option

9 A slider lets you change a variable's value from the stage. Right-click on each readout and select **slider** from the pop-up menu. The **Colour** slider alters the splotches' colour. The **Width** slider makes them spread out or cluster together. Run the project and experiment with the sliders.

Slider Range

Min: 0

Max: 200

OK   Cancel

10 To ensure you have the greatest range of colours to use, right-click on the **Colour** slider and select **set slider min and max**. Change the values in the **Slider Range** box to 0 (minimum) and 200 (maximum), then click **OK**.

Click here for the backdrop library

11 Lastly, go to the stage info area, at the bottom-left of the Scratch editor. Click on the **Choose backdrop from library** symbol. Select "stars" in the library and hit **OK**. Now you're all set to make it a colourful night! Happy skywriting!

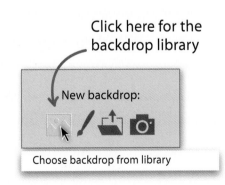

New backdrop:

Choose backdrop from library

Show what you know
Can you write the right answers to these puzzling problems?

1. What is a variable? ....

2. In which section do you find the variable blocks? ....

3. Why do you check the box next to a variable? ....

....

4. What does a slider do? ....

....

5. In which section do you find **stamp** and **clear**? ....

....

6. What is the **stamp** block for? ....

7. What is the **clear** block for? ....

8. In an **if-then** block there is a question at the top and some blocks inside.
Use these words to complete the sentences below: **skips   runs**

    a. If the answer to the question is true (yes), then Scratch

    .... the blocks inside the **if-then** block.

    b. If the answer to the question is false (no), then Scratch

    .... the blocks inside the **if-then** block.

9. If you added the script below to the Ball sprite, what would pressing the
space bar do? ....

```
when  space ▼  key pressed
set  color  to      pick random ⓪ to ⑳⓪
```

↖ Try it out in Scratch to
see if you're right

10. The range of the **Width** slider goes from 0 to 100. This leads to very
spread-out paint. Can you describe the steps to change the range to **0 to 30**
and make the splotches closer together?

a. ....

b. ....

c. ....

d. ....

Quiz time!

Scratch Cat knows his times tables—but do you? In this tricky quiz, he fires questions at you from a glamorous, spotlit stage. Click the green flag to see if you can handle the pressure!

What you'll learn:
• How to ask questions and handle answers
• Advanced block stacking
• How to use **join** blocks to link words or variables
• How an **if-then-else** block works

This background is called "spotlight-stage"

Questions appear in a speech bubble

Use the green flag and red button to start and stop the quiz

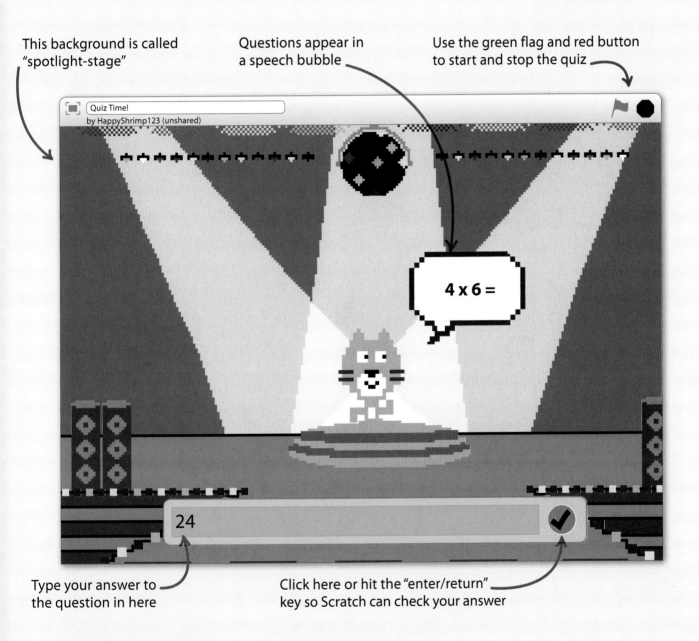

Type your answer to the question in here

Click here or hit the "enter/return" key so Scratch can check your answer

▲ What you do

Scratch Cat will ask you ten fiendish questions about your 1 to 12 times tables. Type your answers into the bar at the bottom of the stage for him to check. You score a point for each answer you get right. Test yourself: can you get ten out of ten?

A script for Quizmaster Scratch Cat

This project has only one script. It's a long, complicated script, and you can't try out the project until the script is complete. But it contains everything Scratch Cat needs to quiz you and keep track of the score.

The spotlight's on me!

Click here to open the backdrop library

1 Start a new project, "Quiz Time!" Click the **Choose backdrop from library** symbol in the stage info area, at the bottom-left of the Scratch editor. Select "spotlight-stage" in the library and click **OK**. Using the mouse, place the cat on top of the spotlit steps.

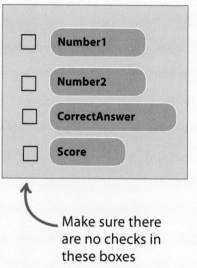

New backdrop:

Choose backdrop from library

2 Click on the cat sprite below the stage, then click on the **Scripts** tab. Before we build any code, we need to create four variables. Call them **"Number1," "Number2," "CorrectAnswer,"** and **"Score."** Uncheck their check boxes so they don't appear on the stage.

☐ Number1

☐ Number2

☐ CorrectAnswer

☐ Score

Make sure there are no checks in these boxes

3 Put this group of blocks together to build the first part of the script. It randomly selects two numbers from 1 to 12 to multiply together. Then it works out the correct answer.

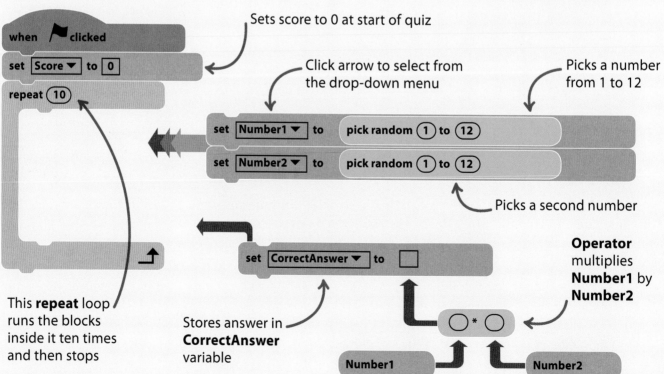

Sets score to 0 at start of quiz

when ⚑ clicked

set Score ▼ to 0

repeat 10

Click arrow to select from the drop-down menu

Picks a number from 1 to 12

set Number1 ▼ to pick random 1 to 12

set Number2 ▼ to pick random 1 to 12

Picks a second number

set CorrectAnswer ▼ to ☐

Operator multiplies **Number1** by **Number2**

This **repeat** loop runs the blocks inside it ten times and then stops

Stores answer in **CorrectAnswer** variable

○ * ○

Number1   Number2

Reminder: "join"

The green **join** block from the **Operators** section links two values together and reports the result, such as joining words and variables to form a sentence.

| join | hello | world |

4 Now create this stack of blocks. It takes the numbers stored in the variables and uses them to ask a multiplication question.

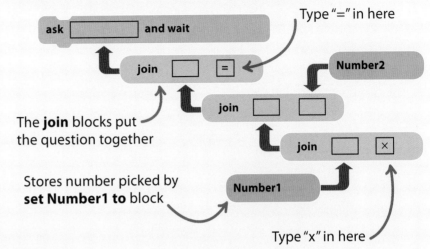

Type "=" in here

The **join** blocks put the question together

Stores number picked by **set Number1 to** block

Type "x" in here

5 Next, make this stack of blocks. It will make Scratch Cat tell you your score out of ten at the end of the quiz.

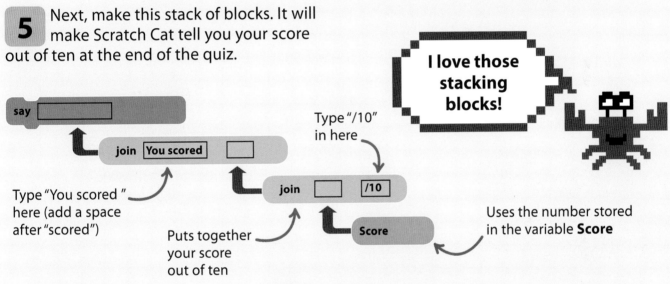

Type "/10" in here

Type "You scored " here (add a space after "scored")

Puts together your score out of ten

Uses the number stored in the variable **Score**

I love those stacking blocks!

6 Insert the **ask** block into the **repeat** loop, after the three **set to** blocks. Then add the **say** block at the end of the script, outside the loop.

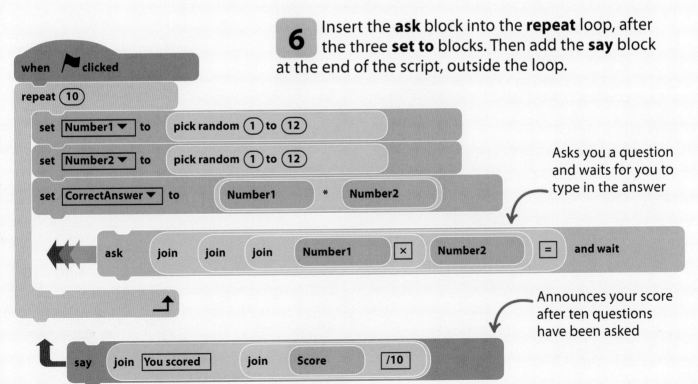

Asks you a question and waits for you to type in the answer

Announces your score after ten questions have been asked

7 You also need to make this section of code. Put it in the **repeat** loop, after the **ask** block. If you type in the right answer, the cat says "Correct!" and a point is added to your score. If not, the cat says "Wrong!" and tells you the correct answer.

This **answer** block stores what you type

Type "Correct!" into this block's window

Answer shows on the stage for 2 seconds

Type "Wrong! Answer is " here (include a space after "is")

8 Your script is now complete and should look like this. Run it—does it work OK? If it doesn't, check that you have all the correct blocks in the correct order. Challenge your friends to see who's the multiplication master!

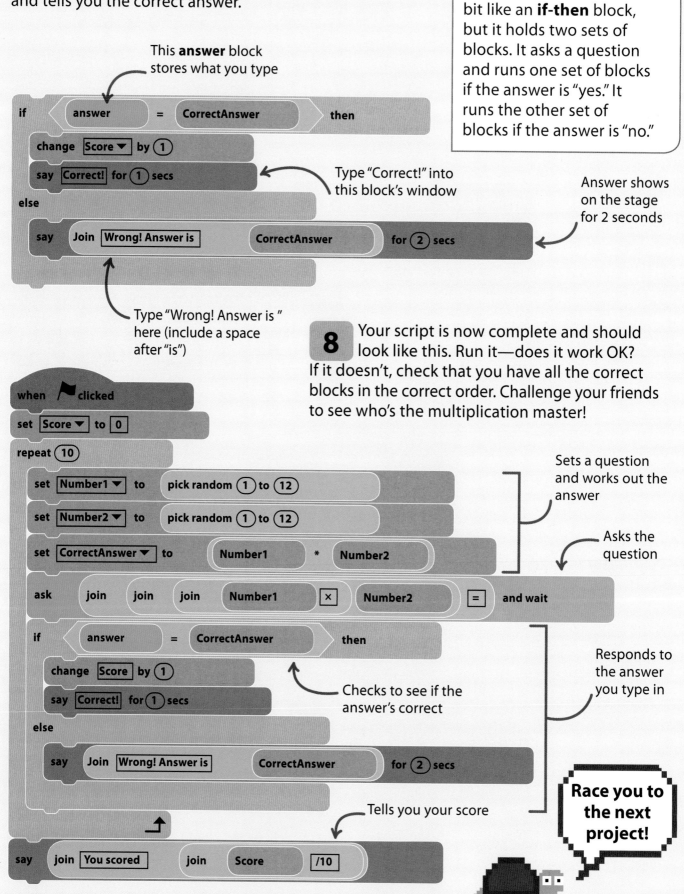

Sets a question and works out the answer

Asks the question

Checks to see if the answer's correct

Responds to the answer you type in

Tells you your score

Race you to the next project!

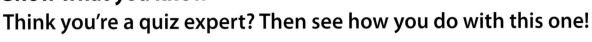

Show what you know
Think you're a quiz expert? Then see how you do with this one!

1. Can you match these Scratch **Operator** blocks to the calculations they show? Draw a line from each block to the correct word.

(15)/(3)   (3) * (4)   (17) + (2)   (9) - (4)

a. Add   **b.** Subtract   **c.** Divide   **d.** Multiply

2. How could you make the quiz questions go all the way up to **20 × 20**?

....

3. How could you stop the easy **1 ×** or **× 1** questions from appearing?

....

4. How could you increase the number of questions in the quiz to **20**?

....

....

5. When you reply to a question in an **ask** block, where does Scratch store what you type in? ....

6. Where could you put these blocks in the code opposite to play a high note for a correct answer and a low note for an incorrect answer?

a. play note (90 ▼) for (0.5) beats   **b.** play note (20 ▼) for (1.0) beats

a. ....

b. ....

7. Can you draw arrows to show where each bit of code should go to make Scratch Cat greet you with your name?

when ▶ clicked   join ☐ ☐   **Hello**

ask │ What's your name │ and wait   say ☐   answer

Pet party

Give your pet a makeover with this crazy project! Pet Party is a ton of fun, and it teaches you some useful Scratch skills—especially how to make your own sprites.

Get your pet in the party mood by dragging a colourful hat onto his head!

The eyes swivel to point toward the mouse-pointer

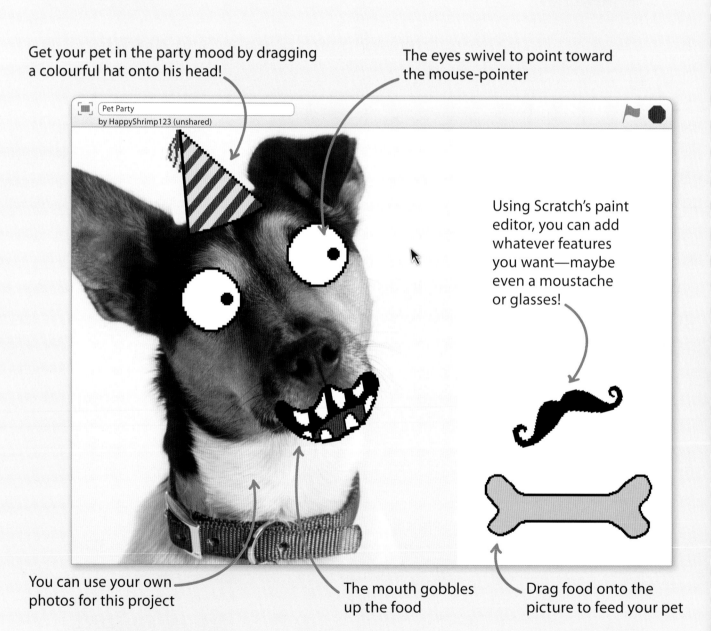

Using Scratch's paint editor, you can add whatever features you want—maybe even a moustache or glasses!

You can use your own photos for this project

The mouth gobbles up the food

Drag food onto the picture to feed your pet

▲ What you do

In this project, you'll draw sprites and use them to add funny features, such as swivelling eyes and a silly party hat, to a photo of a pet or other animal. You'll also be able to feed your pet and watch it gulp down food noisily!

Make some funny features

Let's start by giving your pet some big, googly eyes and a fancy party hat to wear.

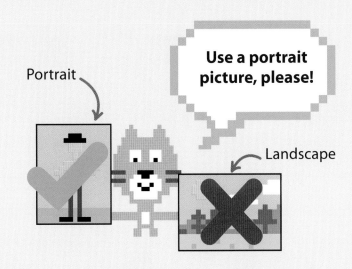

Portrait

Use a portrait picture, please!

Landscape

1 First, take a photo of your pet using a camera or a phone. Make it a portrait (upright) photo, not a landscape (horizontal) one. Upload the photo from your camera or phone to your computer. You may need to ask a parent to help you.

2 Start a new Scratch project called "Pet Party." Go to the sprite list and delete Scratch Cat. Then click on **Upload sprite from file** (the file symbol). Select the picture of your pet and click **OK**. Your pet will appear in the sprite list.

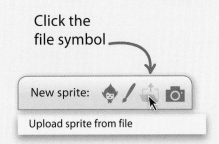

Click the file symbol

New sprite:

Upload sprite from file

3 If your photo title is just a number, you'll need to rename your pet sprite. Select it and click on the blue **(i)** in its top corner. Type your pet's name into the window of the sprite's information panel.

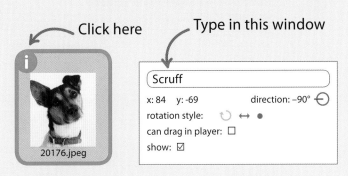

Click here

Type in this window

Scruff

x: 84   y: -69   direction: −90°
rotation style: ↻   ↔   ●
can drag in player: ☐
show: ☑

20176.jpeg

4 Using the mouse, click and drag the photo to the left-hand side of the stage. Leave room on the right for the bone and the hat.

5 To draw the eyes, first click on **Paint new sprite** (the paintbrush symbol) at the top of the sprite list to open the paint editor.

Click here to draw a new sprite

New sprite:

Paint new sprite

Picture problems

If you don't have a pet or you don't have a camera or a phone to take a photo, ask a parent to help you find a copyright-free animal photo on the Internet that's in the public domain. Alternatively, you can draw or trace a picture of an animal, scan it, and save it on your computer.

These new eyes are fantastic!

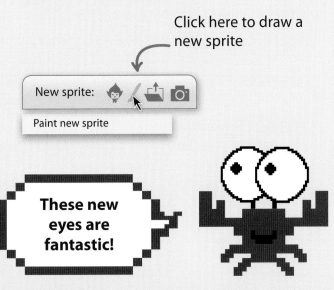

6 Check that **Bitmap Mode** is selected in the bottom-right corner of the paint editor (see below), and that black is selected on the colour palette.

7 Next, click the circle tool on the left-hand side of the paint editor. Make sure the outline shape (rather than solid colour) is selected in the bottom-left corner.

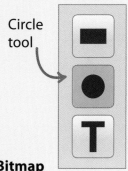

Circle tool

Select the outline shape

Choose black to draw the eyes

Should say **Bitmap Mode** here

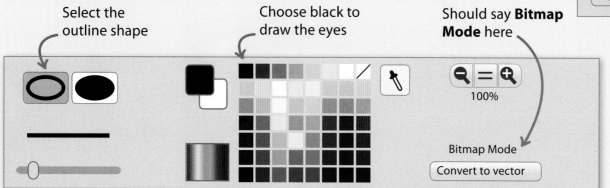

Bitmap Mode

Convert to vector

100%

8 While holding down the shift key, click and drag the mouse to draw a circle. Select the **Fill with color** tool (the paint pot) and choose white on the colour palette. Click on the eye to make it white. To add a pupil, select the circle tool, the solid-colour shape, and black on the palette. Draw a small circle inside the eye, close to the edge, in the "3 o'clock" position.

Fill with color tool

Draw the pupil at "3 o'clock"

Fill the eye with white

9 To make the eye turn properly, you need to centre it. Select the **Set costume center** tool (in the top-right corner of the paint editor), then click in the very centre of the eye.

Set costume center tool

Click in the centre of the eye sprite

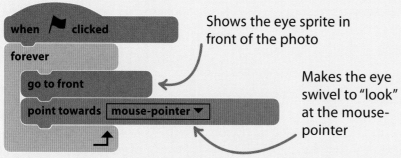

when 🚩 clicked

forever

go to front

point towards mouse-pointer ▼

Shows the eye sprite in front of the photo

Makes the eye swivel to "look" at the mouse-pointer

10 Add this script to the eye sprite. It tells the eye to point at the mouse-pointer, wherever the mouse-pointer is on the stage.

11 Right-click the eye sprite and select **duplicate** from the drop-down menu that appears. This will make a copy of the eye and its script.

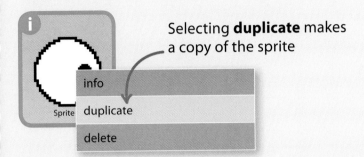

Selecting **duplicate** makes a copy of the sprite

13 Now click the flag to run the eye scripts. Both eyes should swivel to follow the mouse-pointer as you move it around the stage.

If the eyes don't swivel, check your script

15 In the sprite list, select the hat and click on the blue **(i)** in its top corner. Rename the sprite "Hat." Check the **can drag in player** box in the information panel, so you can drag the hat onto your pet's head.

Sends the hat to the right-hand side of the stage

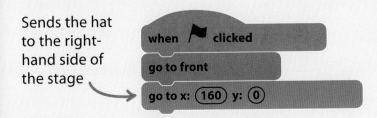

12 Click and drag the eyes into position on the picture. If you're not happy with their size, use the **Grow** and **Shrink** tools on the bar along the top of the Scratch editor to make them bigger or smaller.

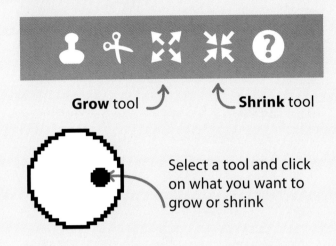

Grow tool   **Shrink** tool

Select a tool and click on what you want to grow or shrink

14 Open the paint editor again by clicking on **Paint new sprite** (the paintbrush). Make another new sprite—the hat. When you've finished, centre your sprite (see step 9).

Use the **Brush** tool to make tassels

Use the **Line** tool to make stripes

Use the paint pot to fill in colours

Checking here lets you drag the hat around in full-screen mode

16 Give the hat this code. The numbers, or coordinates, tell the hat where to appear on the stage at the start. Click the flag to try it out.

It's feeding time!

Your pet's tummy is rumbling. You'll need to draw some food for it to eat and a mouth so that your pet can gobble up the food with a "chomp!"

17 Click on **Paint new sprite** again to draw a food sprite. It could be a bone for a dog, a carrot for a horse, or lettuce for a rabbit. Centre the sprite (see step 9), then rename it.

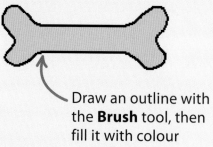

Draw an outline with the **Brush** tool, then fill it with colour

18 Drag the brown **broadcast and wait** block into the food sprite's scripts area. Click on the arrow in the window and select **new message** from the drop-down menu. Then type "Eat" into the pop-up box. Click **OK**.

Type "Eat" here

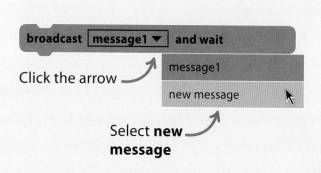

Click the arrow

Select **new message**

New Message

Message name: Eat

OK   Cancel

19 Build this script for the food sprite—in this case, the bone. Run the project. When you drag and drop the food onto the picture, the script should make the food vanish and send the message "Eat" to the mouth sprite. (We'll make the mouth sprite next.)

Sends the food to the bottom-right corner of the stage

This block keeps the food in the corner until you "pick it up" with the mouse-pointer

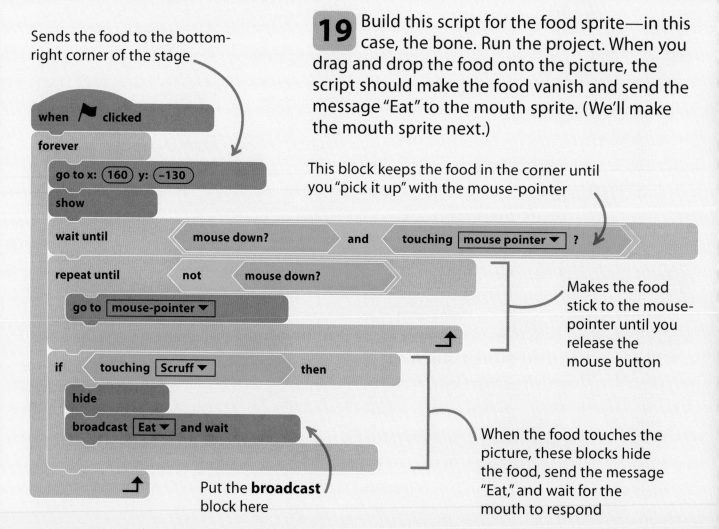

Makes the food stick to the mouse-pointer until you release the mouse button

When the food touches the picture, these blocks hide the food, send the message "Eat," and wait for the mouth to respond

Put the **broadcast** block here

20 Now draw another new sprite—your pet's mouth. The sprite can be just a mouth shape. If you're skilled at drawing sprites, you can try adding teeth and a tongue. Rename the sprite and drag it into position on the picture.

You've got great teeth!

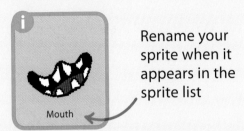

Rename your sprite when it appears in the sprite list

Clicking on the speaker under the **Sounds** tab will take you to the sound library

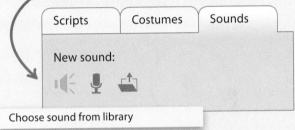

Choose sound from library

21 Let's add an eating sound to the mouth. With the mouth selected, go to the **Sounds** tab and click **Choose sound from library** (the speaker symbol). In the library, select "chomp" and then hit **OK**.

22 Build this code for the mouth. When the script receives the message "Eat," it plays the sound of eating and makes the mouth look as though it's swallowing the food, which disappears. Congratulations—you've completed Pet Party! Click the flag to try it out. Why not make your own funny features to add to the project?

Click on the arrow and select "Eat"

Click on the arrow and select "chomp"

Type "0.1" into the window of each **wait** block

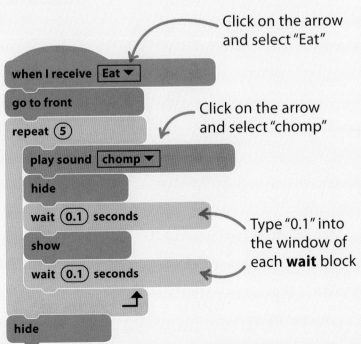

New skill: Messages

Scratch sprites can use messages to "talk" to each other.

This block broadcasts (sends out) a message that tells other sprites to do something.

broadcast Eat ▼ and wait

This block tells other sprites to do something but waits until they finish before continuing.

This block runs any script below it when it receives a particular broadcast message.

Show what you know
Your pet is ready to party—but are *you* ready to take this test?

1. The **when I receive** block will only run the script below it when it gets a message from a .... block.

2. The .... is where you draw new sprites.

3. You can resize sprites using the .... and .... tools.

4. Which block makes a sprite disappear from the stage? ....

5. If you draw your eye like this in the paint editor, what will happen when you run its script? Try your ideas out in Scratch.

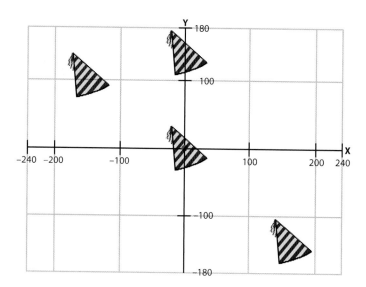

Pupil in centre of eye

Pupil at "7 o'clock position"

Eye sprite not centred correctly

a.   b.   c.

a. ....

b. ....

c. ....

6. You used coordinates in the **go to x: y:** block of the hat's script to position the hat on the stage. Draw lines to link these hats with their coordinates.

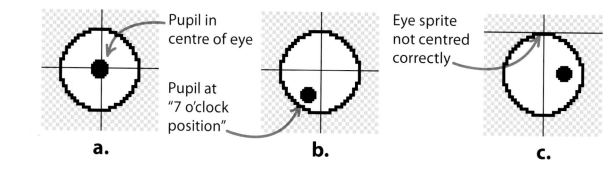

A. (0, 0)

B. (160, −130)

C. (0, 130)

D. (−150, 100)

7. How would you make a short script to add to Scruff the dog sprite so that he barks when he's clicked on?

Bounce painting

Scratch has a magic pen that can draw lines wherever a sprite goes. In this project, you'll create two balls that bounce around the stage drawing beautiful, changing patterns.

What you'll learn:
• That Scratch has a pen that can draw lines when a sprite moves
• That local variables let identical copies of sprites store different data

This project looks great full-screen!

The two balls bounce around the stage

Each time the balls move a step, a coloured line is drawn between them

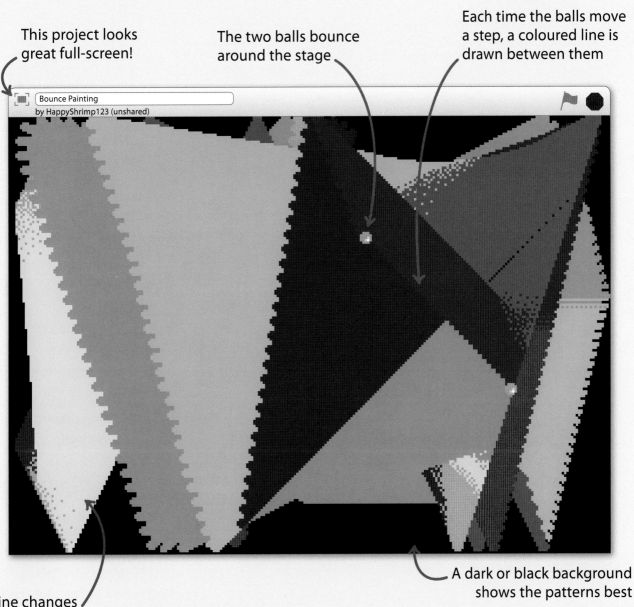

Bounce Painting
by HappyShrimp123 (unshared)

The line changes colour each time to create multicoloured patterns

A dark or black background shows the patterns best

▲ What you do

You simply click the green flag to set the balls in motion. They always set off with a random speed and direction, so you never get the same pattern twice. After a while, the screen fills up, so the project has a script to clear the stage.

Get the balls bouncing!

We'll start by getting the balls bouncing around the stage. They won't paint any patterns just yet—we'll sort that out later.

1 Start a new project called "Bounce Painting." Delete the cat sprite, then load the sprite "Ball" from the library.

Ball

2 Go to the orange **Data** blocks and click on **Make a variable**. Type "Speed" in the pop-up window. Select **For this sprite only**, then click **OK**. When it appears in the **Data** section, uncheck its check box so it doesn't show on the stage.

New Variable

Variable name: Speed

○ For all sprites   ● For this sprite only

OK   Cancel

Click this option

3 Make this script for the ball. Click on the **broadcast** block's arrow and select **new message**. Type "Go" into the pop-up window and click **OK**.

when ⚑ clicked
broadcast Go ▼

Tells the **when I receive** block to run its script

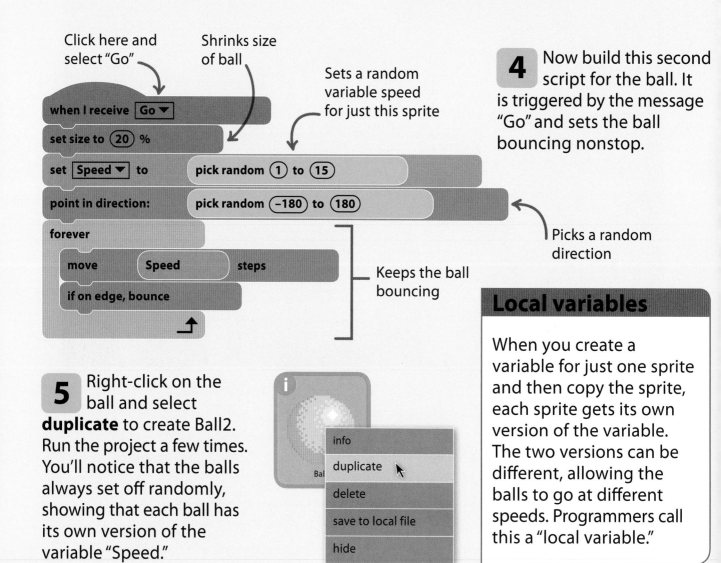

Click here and select "Go"

Shrinks size of ball

Sets a random variable speed for just this sprite

when I receive Go ▼
set size to 20 %
set Speed ▼ to   pick random 1 to 15
point in direction: pick random -180 to 180
forever
    move Speed steps
    if on edge, bounce

4 Now build this second script for the ball. It is triggered by the message "Go" and sets the ball bouncing nonstop.

Picks a random direction

Keeps the ball bouncing

5 Right-click on the ball and select **duplicate** to create Ball2. Run the project a few times. You'll notice that the balls always set off randomly, showing that each ball has its own version of the variable "Speed."

Ball

info
duplicate
delete
save to local file
hide

Local variables

When you create a variable for just one sprite and then copy the sprite, each sprite gets its own version of the variable. The two versions can be different, allowing the balls to go at different speeds. Programmers call this a "local variable."

Drawing lines, tidying up

The next task is to draw the coloured line between the balls. Then we'll darken the backdrop. Finally, we'll make a script to clear the stage when it gets full.

6 Click on **Paint new sprite** to create a new, empty sprite that will draw the line. Call it "Line Draw." We don't need to see this sprite, so we won't draw a costume!

The new sprite doesn't need a costume

Line Draw

7 Add this script to the Line Draw sprite. It draws a coloured line between the two balls, but it also changes the line's colour a little each time. Run the project to test it.

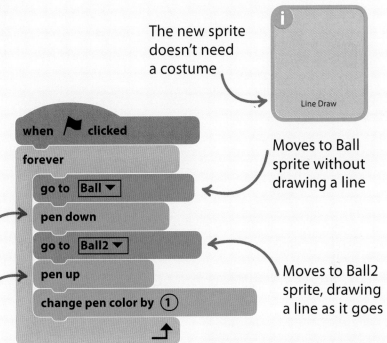

when ⚑ clicked

forever

go to Ball ▼

pen down

go to Ball2 ▼

pen up

change pen color by ①

Moves to Ball sprite without drawing a line

Moves to Ball2 sprite, drawing a line as it goes

Starts drawing a line wherever the Line Draw sprite goes

Stops drawing a line

8 Click on the backdrop in the stage info area, then on the **Backdrops** tab. In the paint editor, select the **Fill with color** tool (the paint pot). Choose a dark colour or black, then click on the drawing area to fill it.

Click here to select the backdrop

1

backdrop1
480x360

Totally random!

9 After a while, the stage gets messy. Add this script to the Line Draw sprite. It clears the stage every now and then, ready for a new pattern. Click the flag to see how it works. That's it—you're finished. Time to get painting!

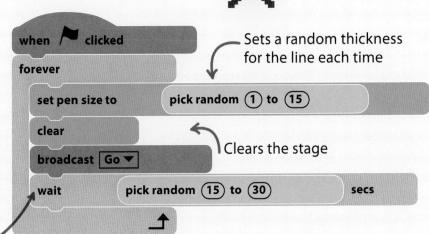

when ⚑ clicked

forever

set pen size to   pick random ① to ⑮

clear

broadcast Go ▼

wait   pick random ⑮ to ㉚   secs

Sets a random thickness for the line each time

Clears the stage

Resets the drawing every 15 to 30 seconds

Show what you know
Get your brain cells bouncing with these tricky questions!

1. Draw a line to link each pen block to its correct meaning.

`pen down`	Clear all pen drawing off the stage
`pen up`	Start drawing as the sprite moves
`set pen size to ③`	Stop drawing as the sprite moves
`clear`	Set how wide the pen line is

2. What would the sprite be called if we duplicated Ball2? ....

3. With three balls, where would you put these two **go to** blocks into the script below to make it draw triangles instead of lines?

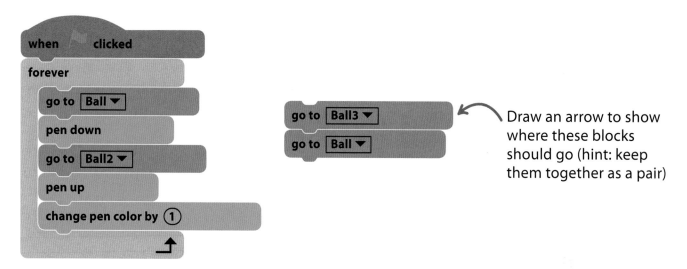

Draw an arrow to show where these blocks should go (hint: keep them together as a pair)

4. How would you get the lines to change colour ten times quicker?

....

5. What happens if you add a **change shade by 10** pen block into the script below the **change pen color** block? ....

....

6. Select each ball sprite one by one, go to the **Data** section, and check the check box of its speed variable. Run the project. What do you notice?

....

....

Solutions

Well done, you've completed all the tasks! Time to check your "Show what you know" answers. How did you do? Are you a Scratch genius now?

We know all the answers!

pages 6–7 What is Scratch?

1. A **script** is a set of instructions (program) in Scratch.

2. Objects that perform actions in a project are called **sprites**.

3. In a Scratch program, the action takes place on the **stage**.

4. Starting a program is called **running** it.

5. A collection of sounds or graphics is called a **library**.

---

pages 14–15 Your first project

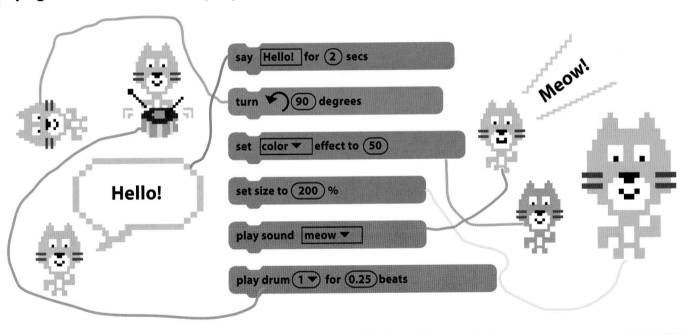

pages 16–17 Move it!

1. What colour are the **Motion** blocks? **dark blue**

2. Scratch measures distances in units called **steps**.

2a. How many of these units wide is the stage? **480**

2b. How many of these units tall is the stage? **360**

3. A mistake in a program is known as a "bug." This script should make the cat move across the stage slowly, but when I click the green flag to run it, nothing happens! What's wrong?

The "when green flag clicked" block is missing.

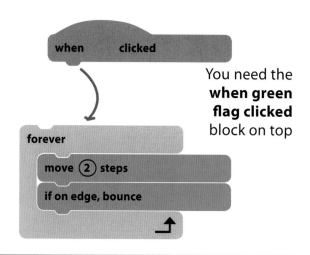

You need the **when green flag clicked** block on top

---

pages 18–19 Which way?

1. What number should replace the **?** in this block to set the sprite's direction to:

Up = **0**   Left = **−90**

Down = **180**   Right = **90**

2. Test your Scratch script reading powers! What does this script do? Read it carefully and try to act each block out in your mind.

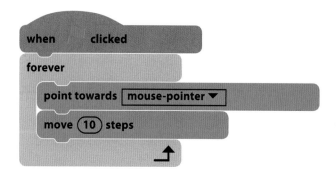

The script makes the cat run toward the mouse-pointer on the stage.

---

pages 20–21 Loops

1. Loops are used to **repeat** groups of blocks.

2. Two types of Scratch loops are **forever** and **repeat**.

3. You can stop a forever loop by clicking the **red button**.

4. In which section do you find the pink blocks? **Sound**

5. Which block section has the loops in? **Control**

6. Bug hunt! This script should draw the four sides of a square, but nothing happens when it's run. Can you spot and suggest a fix for the bug? Programmers call this "debugging."

The repeat loop doesn't say how many repeats to do. Type "4" into its window to fix the bug.

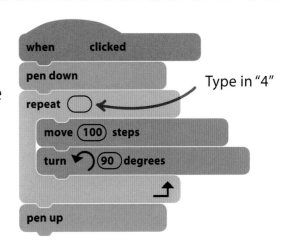

Type in "4"

---

pages 22–23 Animation

1. A different picture a sprite can show on the stage is a **costume**.

2. Animation is showing pictures with slight differences in order to make a sprite appear to move.

3. Can you rearrange the sprites below to animate a jumping pony? Write the numbers 1 to 5 in the boxes to show the correct order.

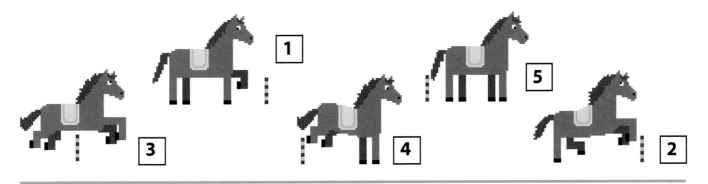

---

pages 24–25 Party time!

1. A background picture on the stage is called a **backdrop**.

2. Circle the block that plays a whole sound before continuing:

3. True or false?

a. A project can have only one backdrop loaded. **False**

b. Only the sprite that loaded a sound can play it. **True**

c. The stage can have sounds and scripts. **True**

d. Once you've chosen a backdrop for a script, you can't change it. **False**

e. A sprite can use a script to change the stage's backdrop. **True**

---

pages 26–27 if-then

This script should make the sprite change colour when you press the space key, but the sprite changes colour all the time. Can you spot the "bug"? **The "change color effect by 25" block needs to go inside the "if-then" block.**

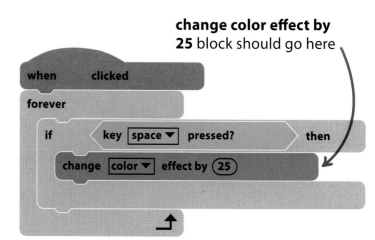

change color effect by 25 block should go here

---

pages 28–29 Variables

1. A variable has a name and a **value**.

2. Make a Variable button is found in the orange **Data** blocks section.

3. Fill in the speech bubbles for these sets of blocks:

Orange variable block makes the dog say "Spot!" (the value of the variable **name**)

If you type in "name" he'll just say "name"!

(Always use the orange variable block to get a variable's value.)

pages 30–31 Math

1. You are the computer! Calculate the values of these blocks.

13 **19** **4** **11** **30** **3**

2. These blocks use variables. Can you work out the answers?

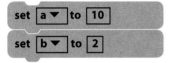

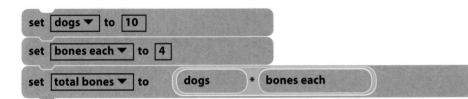

8 **9** **12** **20** **−8** **20** **2** **5**

3. Write down the values stored in these variables.

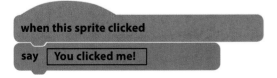

dogs: **10**
bones each: **4**
total bones: **40**

---

pages 32–33 Input and events

1. Which blue **Sensing** block makes a sprite ask a question? **ask**

2. Which block holds the reply given to the question? **answer**

3. Something that happens to the computer, like a mouse click or a key press, is called an **event**.

4. What happens if I click a sprite with this script?

when this sprite clicked

say **You clicked me!**

The sprite says: "You clicked me!"

5. Can more than one script be running at once? **Yes. (Many scripts can run on many sprites—all at once.)**

pages 34–35 if-then-else

1. What shape blocks go into the **condition** window of an **if-then** or **if-then-else** block?

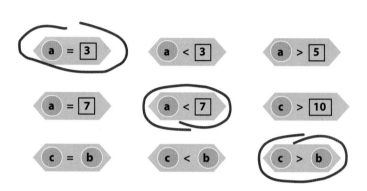

Circle the correct shape

2. Look at the variables below, then circle the green operator blocks that have the value "true."

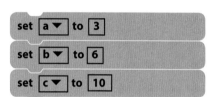

---

pages 36–37 A game: Dragon!

1. Why do we leave the check box on the **score** variable checked?
The box is checked so the score is shown on the stage.

2. How could you make the dragon go at half speed at the start?
Change "set speed 10" to "set speed 5."

3. Which block could you add inside the cat's **forever** loop to make it look like it's walking? **The "next costume" block from "Looks."**

4. How many costumes does the dragon have? **2 (You might want to try altering the game script so that the dragon changes costumes when it touches the cat.)**

5. What would happen if you right-clicked the dragon on the sprite list and chose **duplicate**?
You'd find yourself being chased by TWO dragons, and that would make the game very hard!

pages 40–49 Fishball

1.

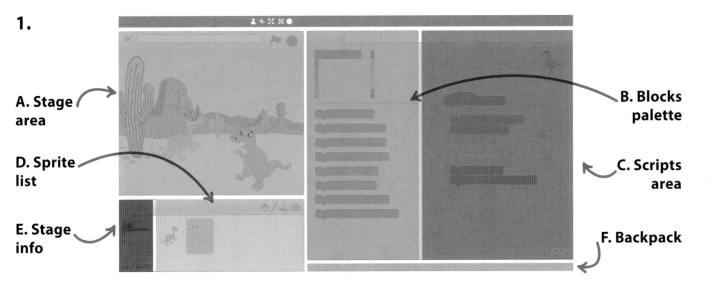

A. Stage area

D. Sprite list

E. Stage info

B. Blocks palette

C. Scripts area

F. Backpack

2. A **forever loop** repeats the blocks inside it nonstop.

3. An **if-then** block either skips or runs the blocks inside it.

4. A **variable** is a block that stores data.

5.

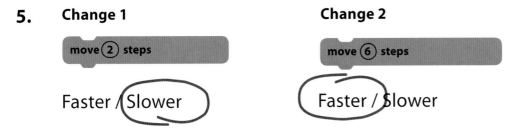

Change 1

move 2 steps

Faster / Slower

Change 2

move 6 steps

Faster / Slower

6. To make the ball move slower, change the number in each of its three **move** blocks to less than 10. For example, if you type in 5, the ball will move at half the speed.

move 10 steps

Any number less than 10 will slow the ball down

7. To lengthen the game to 40 seconds, change both values of 30 in the timing script to 40. To make the game shorter, type in values less than 30.

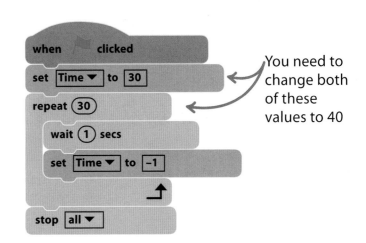

when ▢ clicked

set Time ▼ to 30

repeat 30

    wait 1 secs

    set Time ▼ to -1

stop all ▼

You need to change both of these values to 40

pages 50–55 Ghost hunt

1. Coordinates are always written **(x, y)**.

2. A. (200, 50)   **B.** (−150, 100)   **C.** (200, −150)   **D.** (−50, −100)

3. The ×'s you drew should be in roughly the same positions as the red ×'s shown here.

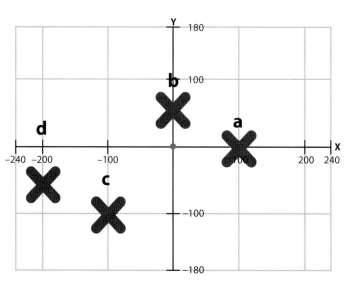

4.

| **Right** | **Down** | **Up** | **Left** |

5.

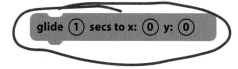

6a. To speed up the ghost, reduce its glide time in the **glide** block.

glide ① secs to x: pick random (−200) to (200) y: pick random (−150) to (150)

↑ If you change this to 0.5 seconds, the ghost will move twice as fast

6b. To slow down the witch, reduce the 10 and −10 steps in her **change x by** and **change y by** blocks to smaller values, such as 5 and −5.

7. Put the **point in direction 90** block in the witch's right arrow **if-then** block. The **point in direction −90** block goes in her left arrow **if-then** block.

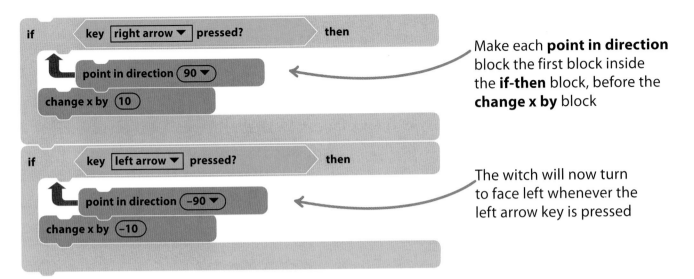

if ⟨ key [right arrow ▼] pressed? ⟩ then

  point in direction (90 ▼)

change x by (10)

Make each **point in direction** block the first block inside the **if-then** block, before the **change x by** block

if ⟨ key [left arrow ▼] pressed? ⟩ then

  point in direction (–90 ▼)

change x by (–10)

The witch will now turn to face left whenever the left arrow key is pressed

You'll notice that the poor witch now spends half her time upside down! To fix this, select her in the sprite list, click on the blue **(i)** and change her rotation style to left–right.

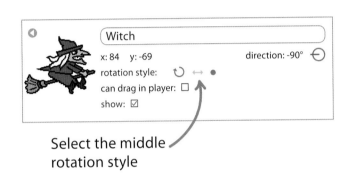

Witch

x: 84 y: -69   direction: -90°

rotation style: ↻ ↔ ●

can drag in player: ☐

show: ☑

Select the middle rotation style

---

pages 56–61 Rapid reaction

1. You can resize sprites using the **Grow** and **Shrink** tools above the stage, at the top of the Scratch screen.

2. The "scissors" symbol is the delete tool from the bar above the stage.

3. The **timer** block is found in the **Sensing** section of the blocks palette.

4. False: unchecking a variable's check box will *hide* the variable, not show it.

5. The coordinates **x:0, y:0** mark the dead centre of the stage.

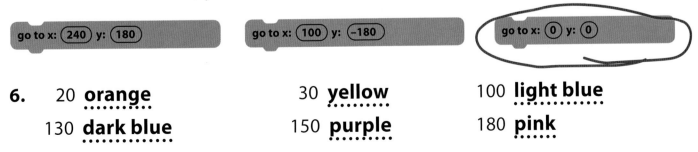

go to x: (240) y: (180)   go to x: (100) y: (–180)   go to x: (0) y: (0)

6.   20 **orange**   30 **yellow**   100 **light blue**

       130 **dark blue**   150 **purple**   180 **pink**

7.

a **is more than** b   c **is less than** d   d **equals** e

8. Put the **play sound** blocks inside the players' **if-then** blocks. Don't forget you'll need to load these two sounds from the library if you want to add this code to your game.

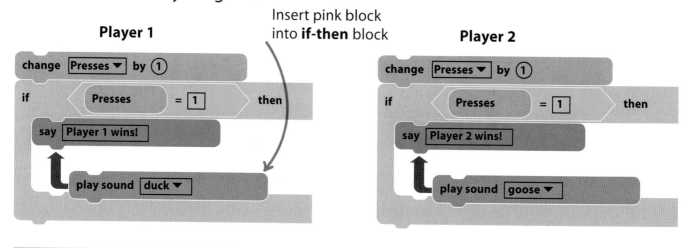

Insert pink block into **if-then** block

Player 1

```
change Presses ▼ by ①
if        Presses        = 1        then
    say Player 1 wins!

        play sound duck ▼
```

Player 2

```
change Presses ▼ by ①
if        Presses        = 1        then
    say Player 2 wins!

        play sound goose ▼
```

---

pages 62–66 Melon bounce

1. **Data** blocks are **orange**

Events blocks are **brown**

Motion blocks are **dark blue**

Operators blocks are **green**

Sound blocks are **pink**

Sensing blocks are **light blue**

Control blocks are **yellow**

Looks blocks are **purple**

2. Quickly switching a sprite's costumes to make it look as if it's walking or running is called **animation**.

3. Making the cat move faster would make the game **easier**.

4. You could make the melons fall faster by increasing the number of steps in their **move 10 steps** blocks.

5. You can make the melons smaller by clicking on them with the **Shrink** tool above the stage. You could also resize them by adding the purple **set size to** block at the start of their scripts. Type in the percentage you want them reduced by.

Get this block from the **Looks** section

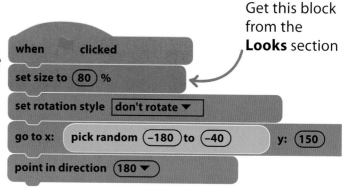

```
when      clicked
set size to (80) %
set rotation style don't rotate ▼
go to x:    pick random (-180) to (-40)      y: (150)
point in direction (180 ▼)
```

6. To add extra melons to the game, select a melon in the sprite list. Then right-click and choose **duplicate** from the pop-up menu that appears.

7. The changes to the melons' **pick random** blocks make two melons keep to the left half of the stage while the other two keep to the right half. This stops all four melons from bunching up together.

8. You can base your music script on the one you built for the Ghost Hunt game. Choose any music you like from the sound library and load it into the cat sprite.

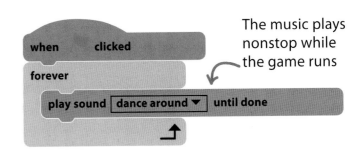

The music plays nonstop while the game runs

---

pages 70–75 Weird music

1. The **Looks** blocks are **Purple.**

2. A **forever loop** repeats the blocks inside it endlessly.

3.

(17) + (2) a. **19**

(9) - (4) b. **5**

(3) * (4) c. **12**

(15) / (3) d. **5**

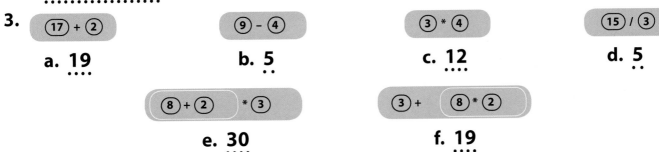

((8) + (2) * (3)) e. **30**

((3) + (8) * (2)) f. **19**

(For parts **e** and **f**, remember to calculate the inner block first, then use the result to calculate the outer block.)

4.

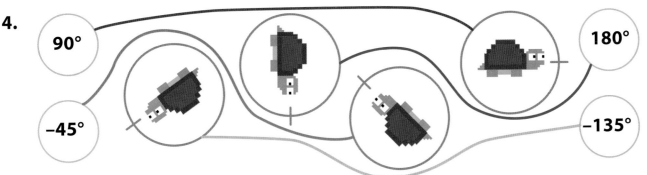

90°   180°

−45°   −135°

5. When you hold down the mouse button, Scratch plays a stream of notes. It stops only when you release the mouse button.

6. When you check the box beside the **volume** block under the **Sounds** tab, a readout for the volume setting appears on the stage.

7. The script picks a random musical instrument each time you press the space bar.

pages 76–80 Skywriting

1. A variable is used to store data in a program.

2. The variable blocks are found in the orange **Data** section, under the **Scripts** tab.

3. You check the box next to a variable to show the variable's name and value on the stage.

4. A slider lets you change the value of a variable from the stage.

5. You'll find the **stamp** and **clear** blocks in the dark green **Pen** section.

6. The **stamp** block leaves an image of a sprite on the stage.

7. The **clear** block removes all the stamps from the stage.

8a. If the answer to the question is true (yes), then Scratch **runs** the blocks inside the **if-then** block.

8b. If the answer to the question is false (no), then Scratch **skips** the blocks inside the **if-then** block.

9. If you add the script to the Ball sprite, Scratch chooses a random colour for the splotches when you press the space bar. If you keep the space bar *and* the mouse key pressed down at the same time, you get a continuous spray of splotches that constantly change colour!

10. To change the range of the **Width** slider from **0 to 30** and make the splotches closer together, you:

a. Right-click on the **Width** slider.

b. Select **set slider min and max**.

c. Type 30 into the **Max** window of the pop-up box.

d. Click **OK**.

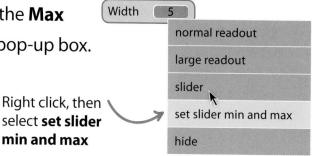

Right click, then select **set slider min and max**

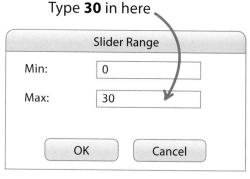

Type **30** in here

pages 81–85 Quiz time!

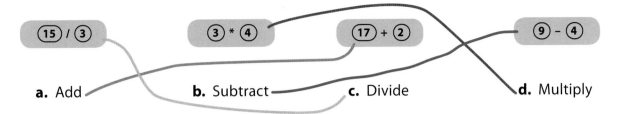

15 / 3   3 * 4   17 + 2   9 - 4

a. Add   **b.** Subtract   **c.** Divide   **d.** Multiply

2. To make the quiz questions go all the way up to **20 × 20**, change the upper limit in each **pick random** block to **20**.

3. To stop the easy **1 ×** or **× 1** questions, change the lower limit in each **pick random** block to **2**.

4. To increase the number of questions in the quiz to **20**, change the 10 at the top of the **repeat** loop to **20**, and the 1/10 in the last **say** block to **1/20**.

5. When you reply to a question in an **ask** block, Scratch stores what you type in an **answer** block.

6a. Make **a** the first block in the **if-then** part of the **if-then-else** block.

6b. Make **b** the first block in the **else** part of the **if-then-else** block.

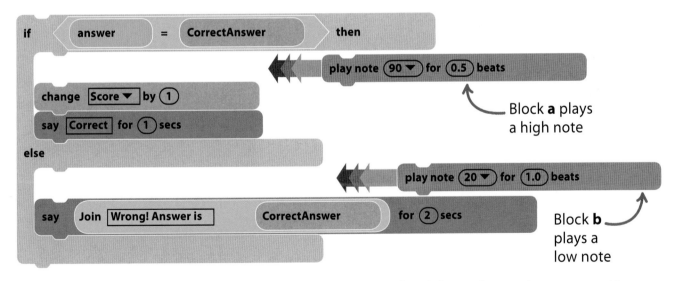

7. This is how you put the blocks together. Try building the script yourself.

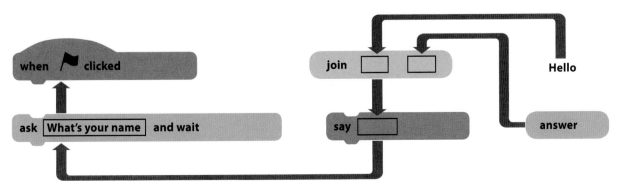

pages 86–92 Pet party

1. The **when I receive** block will only run the script below it when it gets a message from a **broadcast** block.

2. The **paint editor** is where you draw new sprites.

3. You can resize sprites using the **grow** and **shrink** tools.

4. The **hide** block makes a sprite disappear from the stage.

5a. If you draw the pupil in the very centre of the eye, you won't notice the eye swivelling because it will be looking straight out of the picture.

5b. If you draw the pupil at the "7 o'clock" position, rather than "3 o'clock", the eye will turn but it won't appear to follow the mouse-pointer.

5c. If the eye isn't centred correctly, the whole eye will revolve around the centre point, not just the pupil—your poor pet will look very strange!

6.

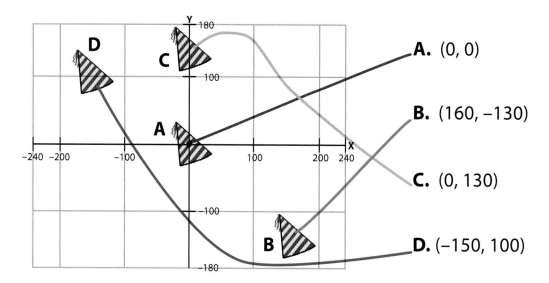

A. (0, 0)

B. (160, –130)

C. (0, 130)

D. (–150, 100)

7. The short script below would make the dog bark when he's clicked on.

You would have to load the sound "dog1" from the library

Build a similar script for your own pet sprite—there are lots of animal noises in the sound library. If your computer contains a microphone or you have one you can plug into it, why not record your own animal sounds? Just click on **Record new sound** (the microphone symbol) under the **Sounds** tab.

pages 93–96 Bounce painting

1. Draw a line to link each pen block to its correct meaning.

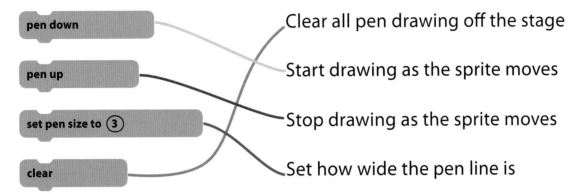

pen down   Clear all pen drawing off the stage

pen up   Start drawing as the sprite moves

set pen size to ③   Stop drawing as the sprite moves

clear   Set how wide the pen line is

2. If you duplicated Ball2, the new sprite would be called **Ball3**.

3. If you put these two extra **go to** blocks between the **go to Ball2** and **pen up** blocks, the three balls would draw triangles.

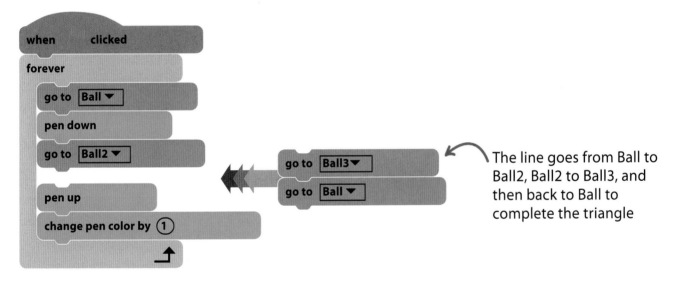

The line goes from Ball to Ball2, Ball2 to Ball3, and then back to Ball to complete the triangle

4. To get the lines to change colour ten times quicker, change the 1 to a **10** in the **change pen color by** block.

5. If you add a **change shade by 10** pen block into the script below the **change pen color by** block, it changes the brightness as well as the colour, so the picture becomes stripey.

6. If you check the check box of each ball's **Speed** variable, the names and speeds of both balls will show on the stage. You'll notice that they move at different speeds, because each ball has its own copy of the variable. Try it for yourself and see.

Glossary

Stuck in Scratch? Click on **Tips** on the menu bar for advice. Or use the **Help tool** ⓘ —click on it, and then click on a block to bring up the help page for that block.

animation
Changing pictures quickly to make something appear to move on the screen.

backdrop
The picture behind the sprites on the stage.

backpack
A way to copy things between Scratch projects.

block
An instruction in Scratch. Blocks can be joined together.

bug
A mistake in a program. It's called a bug because insects got into the wiring of the first computers, causing errors.

condition
A "true or false?" question that is used to make a decision in a computer program.

costume
The picture a sprite shows on the stage.

data
Information—for example, numbers or words.

debug
To remove bugs; to find and fix the errors in a program.

event
Something that happens on the computer, like a mouse click.

input
Data that goes into a program; for example, from the keyboard.

library
A collection of sprites, sounds, or costumes.

loop
An instruction that makes other instructions repeat.

program
A list of instructions that tell a computer what to do.

operator
A block that works something out from data, such as adding two numbers together.

operating system (OS)
The program that controls everything on your computer, such as OS X or Windows.

run
To start a program.

script
A stack of instructions that are run in order.

sprite
A picture on the stage that a script can move and change.

stage
The area containing the sprites, where a Scratch project runs.

string
The word used by programmers for data that contains words.

variable
A place to store data in a program. A variable always has a name and a value.

Note for parents

Help your child work logically through any difficulties. Check for obvious errors, such as swapping similar blocks in scripts. Also check that scripts are controlling the correct sprites. Don't forget that using Scratch should be fun. The Scratch website is run by Massachusetts Institute of Technology (MIT) and is intended to be safe for children to use. Try it yourself!